CLERKS: Please checkout
only 1 monologue book per
patron!!!

True-to-life monolog
characterizations for student actors

Diana Howie

mp

MERIWETHER PUBLISHING LTD.
Colorado Springs, Colorado

Meriwether Publishing Ltd., Publisher
P.O. Box 7710
Colorado Springs, CO 80933

Editor: Theodore O. Zapel
Typesetting: Jennifer Vokolek McAloon
Cover design: Janice Melvin

Library of Congress Cataloging-in-Publication Data

Howie, Diana M.
　　　　Tight Spots : true-to-life monolog characterizations for student actors / Diana M. Howie. --1st ed.
　　　　　　　p.　　　cm.
　　　　　ISBN 1-56608-054-1 (pbk.)
　　　　　　　1. Monologues. 2. Acting--Auditions.　　　I. Title.
　　　　PN2080.H68　　1999
　　　　812'.54--dc21　　　　　　　　　　　　　　　　　　99-36972
　　　　　　　　　　　　　　　　　　　　　　　　　　　　　　　CIP

1　　2　　3　　4　　5　　6　　7　　8　　　　03　　02　　01　　00　　99

Contents

Part Three:
Monologs for Guys (Humorous) 61

Part Four
Monologs for Guys (Serious) 91

Introduction

Tight Spots is a balanced collection of fifty character monologs (twenty-five female, twenty-five male), drawn from real-life experiences of contemporary teens, living in both urban/suburban areas and in small towns. Divorce, parents, school, getting in trouble, finding your own way, physical appearance, the opposite sex — all loom large in these monologs. In each one, the character is saying what is currently on his mind, sometimes speaking to another person, sometimes talking to himself, but almost always anticipating a difficult confrontation, experiencing something frightening or new, or weighing the options.

I didn't write these monologs with any particular agenda or topic in mind — I more or less took down what the individuals' stories were, just as I heard them. Sometimes they were told to me by the person speaking in the monolog, other times passed on to me by a parent or a friend. People sometimes claim that teenagers are so hard to understand because they don't like to say what's on their minds or tell you what's weighing them down. I haven't found that to be true. I have found, however, that adults tend to give advice rather than to just listen to a teen, and that teens don't mind expressing their feelings to adults as long as they don't have to listen to any follow-up advice.

Each piece takes five minutes or less to perform. Simple props are suggested in many of the monologs to help establish the setting. Most props are optional or can be pantomimed if not available. A program could be easily put together by combining however many monologs it takes to fill your allotted time. The age given is the actual age of the teen whose story was the germ of the monolog; many, I think, can be played by a range of ages.

— Diana Howie

Publisher's Note: We have divided the monologs into lighter material that could be considered humorous despite the crisis situation, and heavier, more serious material. However, we agree with the author that most of the monologs contain elements of both.

1

NOTE: The numerals running vertically down the left margin of each page of dialog are for the convenience of the director. With these, he/she may easily direct attention to a specific passage.

Part One:
Monologs
for Girls
(Humorous)

Chocolate Chip Caramel

1   (BILLIE JEAN, 15, wearing an oversized shirt, waiting
2 her turn at an ice-cream counter, talking to another girl
3 waiting to be served)
4   Me? I always get the chocolate chip caramel in the
5 waffle cone. Then I have them put the thick fudge
6 sauce on top. You gotta get the thick fudge sauce.
7 That's the only one that doesn't go through the
8 bottom and run down your arm. Or, you can get the
9 waffle cone with the chocolate coating inside. That's
10 almost as good. I kind of go back and forth, one day
11 the sauce, another day the chocolate cone. Sometimes
12 I have a real hard time deciding which one to have.
13   My boyfriend said I should try the ice cream in a
14 cup. I hated to tell him he was out of his mind, so I
15 didn't say anything. He says I should try some of the
16 other flavors. I told him next year. Maybe. He always
17 asks if I tried the sherbet yet. Or the frozen yogurt. He
18 used to come here with me, but ... I got tired of all his
19 suggestions. He was taking a lot of the fun out of
20 coming here. I don't think he really likes ice cream like
21 I do. He was never the one who suggested that we
22 come here — I always had to bring it up. So, I found
23 a time that I could come by myself. He's at work now.
24   Oh, he's full of other suggestions too. We're
25 supposed to go to this party in two weeks. A moonlight
26 swim party. With a late night candlelight supper
27 around the pool. And dancing. I hope they do those
28 candles that float on the water. Those are sooooo
29 romantic. I was so excited when I got the invitation, I
30 could just see it! Then Frank said, he really wants to

1 see me in a bikini at that party. Now he's got ideas
2 about what I should wear. A two-piece. I don't have a
3 two-piece anymore. When I gained ten pounds, mostly
4 around the middle, I gave a lot of clothes away.
5   So now I'm thinking, maybe I could wear a bikini
6 underneath one of those wrap skirts and a little
7 blouse. Then I could always say, I don't feel like
8 swimming ... yet. I could be cold. I could have a
9 stomachache. There's lots of things I could do to
10 keep that skirt on. I know what I'd look like in a
11 bikini, I see something pretty close to a bikini every
12 morning in the mirror. I've got these love handles.
13 Ever had 'em? *(Beat)* Guess they're pretty common.
14 Frank's always got his fingers on them. He knows
15 they're there, but I don't think he knows what they
16 look like.
17   *(Beat, employee speaks to her.)*
18   Oh! my turn? Uhh ... the usual. Chocolate chip
19 caramel. It'll be a long time 'fore I'm off that. *(Beat)*
20 Gosh, I hadn't decided, we've been so busy talking —
21   *(Beat, interrupted by other customer)*
22   A cup? You like it in a cup? *(Beat)* Oh there can't
23 be that many calories in one little cone! *(Beat)* Huh.
24 Well, are you going to sit and eat yours? Well, well
25 okay, maybe I'll try it too. This once. *(To employee)* A
26 cup, with fudge sauce. *(To other customer)* Is this how
27 you get rid of love handles, by cutting out the
28 cones? *(Beat)* Well, I'll try most anything once. After
29 all, it's the ice cream I really like.
30
31
32
33
34
35

Automatic Suspension

1 (JACKIE, 16, at home, reading, doorbell rings. JACKIE
2 yells to her mother and jumps up, book in hand.)
3 **I'll get it!** (Opens door. Policeman there.) **Hi! You**
4 **collecting for the circus, that circus thing you do, that**
5 **benefit, or whatever it is?** — (Beat, he interrupts.) **Yes,**
6 **yes I'm Jackie.** (Beat) **Yes, Jacquelyn Elaine Bennett.**
7 **How do you know my name?** (Beat, he indicates a slip of
8 paper.) **What's that?** (Beat) **I can't come with you. I**
9 **gotta do homework until supper and after that I'm**
10 **going—**
11 (Beat, interrupted)
12 **No, I don't, I don't understand what that means,**
13 **some kind of summary something—**(Interrupted)
14 **Summons.** (Beat) **Well yeah, sure, I got a warning**
15 **about a month ago.** (Beat) **Yeah, that was it I think, for**
16 **speeding.** (Beat) **Well, about that. Over a hundred,**
17 **okay but, but it was on the Interstate.** (Beat) **No! We**
18 **agreed it was just a warning, it wasn't a ticket.** (Beat)
19 **No, I swear, he didn't give me a ticket, he gave me a**
20 **warning, and I read it—** (Beat, looks at book in her
21 hand.) **Oh yeah, you're right, that is it. Makes a great**
22 **bookmark. Huh?** (Tells her anything in writing is a tick-
23 et.) **Oh. Huh. I guess you could be right, I've had some**
24 **warnings on some other stuff, and I think this is the**
25 **only bookmark I've ever been given.** (Beat) **Gee, I don't**
26 **remember ... following too close, I think, was one, but**
27 **you know, I've never hit anybody.** (Beat) **Oh yeah,**
28 **yeah, I did have an accident. The car kind of rolled**
29 **over and all, but it was just me, nobody else, I didn't**
30 **hit anybody! How'd you know about that anyway?** (He

1   *holds up a file.)* **You got a file on me?**
2   *(She steps outside, closing door behind her.)*
3   **Uh, my mother's not feeling real well today, I'd**
4   **rather not disturb her right now if you don't mind,**
5   **so we'll just talk out here until you're finished.**
6   *(Policeman tells her to come with him. She smiles*
7   *real big.)*
8   **Gee, I can come down to the station tomorrow—**
9   **no, not tomorrow, tomorrow's Wednesday and I've**
10 **got drill team after school, but I can come some**
11 **other day this week.** *(Beat)* **I don't know where that**
12 **is.** *(Beat)* **I'd really rather not go now if you don't**
13 **mind. I hate to just walk off and leave Mother,**
14 **she'd worry— where exactly is the courthouse? I**
15 **could get out of drill team tomorrow if I really have**
16 **to—** *(Beat, interrupted)* **Oh no, don't worry about**
17 **that, I can drive anywhere I want, I'd just prefer not**
18 **to have to—** *(Beat)* **No. No way. That policeman**
19 **definitely didn't tell me that!** *(Beat)* **Where did it say**
20 **that?** *(Looking at her bookmark)* **"Automatic**
21 **suspension of your drivers license upon failure to**
22 **report to the Traffic Court on or before the day of**
23 **your summons. Reinstatement will be granted only**
24 **after appearing in Court."**
25   *(Beat)*
26   **Fifty dollars? Fifty dollars a day for every day**
27 **until I show up? I know I didn't read that!** *(Beat, he's*
28 *pointed something else out on her ticket.)* **Penalties.**
29 **That's an awful long list. Listen, I'll be there. I'll be**
30 **there as soon as I can, I just—** *(Beat, interrupts her-*
31 *self.)* **I gotta tell my folks. I gotta get some money. I**
32 **gotta—**
33   *(Beat, interrupted)*
34   **Well sure, I don't mind signing something for you.**
35 *(Beat)* **I did?** *(Looks at her ticket.)* **Oh. Yeah, I forgot.**

1 *(Beat)* **Fifty dollars already? But when's the dead-**
2 **line—** *(Beat, he interrupts.)* **Yesterday?? But this**
3 **driving business, this thing with my license I —**
4 **Geez! How am I supposed to get there without**
5 **telling everyone about the license and the money**
6 **and—** *(Beat, interrupted)* **Oh. I see. Now I get it. Well,**
7 **okay.** *(Starts walking away, then turns to him follow-*
8 *ing behind her.)* **I don't suppose you can give me a**
9 **ride back, too? Great. Thanks.** *(Walks off.)*
10
11
12
13
14
15
16
17
18
19
20
21
22
23
24
25
26
27
28
29
30
31
32
33
34
35

Fifty-Fifty

1   *(HARRIET, 14, has just received a pile of cash from a*
2 *friend who played the lottery for her, and she is counting it*
3 *and putting it into a zippered bag. Her father walks in.)*
4   **Huh?** *(Turns around.)* **Oh, Dad! I didn't know you**
5 **were home.** *(Beat)* **Huh? Oh yeah, some money. Just,**
6 **uh, putting it away ... I, uh, won't have a chance to get**
7 **to the bank before Saturday, and I don't want to lose it**
8 **by carrying it in my purse and all.**
9   *(Beat)*
10 **Noooo, I didn't rob a bank.** *(Beat)* **It's not all that**
11 **much. A lot of small bills. You know how that can look**
12 **like a lot. It's not so much, really.** *(Beat)* **Three hundred**
13 **dollars.** *(Beat)* **Well ... well ... No! I didn't steal it! I don't**
14 **know anybody to steal three hundred dollars from! I ...**
15 **I ... well, I had somebody buy me a lottery ticket, and I**
16 **won — are you mad?**
17   *(Watches for his reaction, then smiles.)*
18 **Yeah, I thought it was pretty good too. For a first**
19 **time try and all that. Actually it paid three hundred and**
20 **eighty dollars, but I told her I would give her twenty**
21 **percent of whatever I got. So, three hundred. I'm**
22 **going to put mine in the bank, then it'll be there, when**
23 **I need it.**
24   *(Beat)*
25 **No, there's nothing I want to buy, not right now.**
26 **What I really want is one of those little savings books**
27 **like I had before. I really liked going to the bank, giving**
28 **them the book, and seeing how much more I had since**
29 **the last time. Don't you remember doing that with me?**
30 **Don't you remember how much fun it was?**

1   *(Beat, Dad offers to keep it for her.)*
2   I don't think so, Dad. I really want one of those
3   little books. But thanks anyway. And hey, you don't
4   have to go with me this time. I called. I can open the
5   account on my own with just my school i.d. They're
6   even open on Saturday morning. Don't you think
7   that's weird? I'm too young to buy a lottery ticket,
8   but I'm old enough to have my own bank account.
9   *(Dad asks another question.)*
10   Oh Dad, that account hasn't been there for a long
11   time. That was years ago — third grade! *(Beat)* I
12   didn't buy anything, nothing, the amount just kept
13   going up, remember? You and me, we'd go down to
14   the bank every so often, sometimes even to the big
15   one on Main Street, and get the new amount typed
16   into the little book ... You used to say how proud
17   Granddad would be, that we were saving something
18   for once. *(Beat)* It's gone — honest! *(Beat)* I don't
19   remember anymore, some big bill, house insurance,
20   something like that, and you and mom didn't have
21   enough to pay it. I kept the little book for a long time,
22   but there was only a few dollars in the account, and
23   I never had any more to add to it, and after a while I
24   got tired of looking at it, so I went down and took out
25   the rest of the money and threw the book away.
26   *(Beat, laughs.)*
27   Oh yeah? You're going to turn me in? You wouldn't!
28   I don't believe you. *(Beat)* Well ... well, I guess we could.
29   All it takes is a hundred dollars to open the account
30   but, but— *(Beat)* Yeah, I bought the ticket with my
31   allowance. *(Beat)* No, there wouldn't be anything to
32   split now if you hadn't given me the money in the first
33   place. *(Holds out some bills.)* Fifty-Fifty. Okay? Okay.
34
35

The Mall

1   *(NATALIE, age 12, backs onto stage, talking to her aunt*
2 *Off-stage.)*
3   Noooo, that's all right. I'll just stay here and read.
4 No, I'm not sick, I'm fine, really! You go ahead. I
5 wanted to finish my book. No. Please. Don't worry
6 about me. You go. I am not interested in that particular
7 store. Bye. Bye. See you later.
8   *(Shuts door, blows top as soon as she does, exasperat-*
9 *ed with her aunt.)*
10   Ooooooh! Ooooh! Ooooo-ooooo-ooooh! Be nice,
11 Natalie, be nice. Calm down. She didn't mean to do it.
12 She didn't mean to do it to you. She's your favorite
13 aunt, your favorite aunt, things will be fine, you still
14 have a few more days here, you will get to go shopping.
15 Ooo-oooo-oooo-ooooh! Why do they think I came
16 here? Doesn't everyone come to _____ *(Insert name of*
17 *nearby big city.)* to shop? I want to go to all the malls.
18 I want to go to all the stores we don't have at home.
19 I told her the first thing I wanted to do was to go to
20 the _____ *(Insert name of nearby mall.).* She said the
21 traffic there is awful, and that the best thing about
22 shopping here is the incredible discount stores. Well,
23 what can I say. I don't shop discount.
24   I mean, I don't want to hurt her feelings, but I am
25 sure the things I want are not in any discount store.
26 Labels don't show up in discount stores. How could
27 they? There's a price and that's it. Sales, okay, they
28 come along, but not for the really good stuff. She says
29 "no," she finds big labels at discount prices all the
30 time, but I don't think so. She and I don't wear the

1 same kind of thing anyway, so how would she know
2 whether there's any stuff there that I would buy?
3   I should have gone. Should I have gone? Oh I
4 think not. Better to let her know just where I stand
5 or I will never get to the _____ *(Insert name of nearby*
6 *mall.)*. I mean she'll do anything for me, but, well,
7 she doesn't seem to be that interested in shopping.
8 Oh, we've done a little. She got me in some funny
9 ethnic-type place yesterday. We went to the museum,
10 and next door was this little store-like place with
11 clothes from all these little villages somewhere.
12 Weird stuff, mostly folded up, even the dresses. They
13 liked to talk about it all being hand-woven and hand-
14 stitched. Who cares? I haven't seen anything like it
15 in the magazines. My aunt didn't buy anything, but
16 she sure did look it all over. Actually it reminded me
17 of some of the stuff in the museum.
18   I should tell her that I want to go ice skating.
19 That ought to do it. I hear the rink is right smack in
20 the middle of the _____ *(Insert name of nearby mall.)*
21 with the stores all around it. And there's three
22 floors of them! When we get there, well, I'd just
23 have to come up with some excuse. Like, gee, I
24 forgot, I don't know how to skate. No, she's sure to
25 ask me that before we go. Maybe, once I see how
26 big it is, I'm scared? I know, I could be cold, or, my
27 knees could feel funny, oh … I'd better come up with
28 something good or I will never get into a real store.
29 Anything but discount! Discount. I mean really.
30
31
32
33
34
35

I Hate It Here

1   *(SHARON, 15, in a uniform, with a book bag, etc.,*
2 *walks in the door, home from school.)*
3   I hate it here! *(Slams books down.)* **Hate it, hate it,**
4 **hate it!** *(Kicks off shoes, takes off part of uniform that has*
5 *school badge on it, throws it on floor, and then jumps on*
6 *it. When finished, drops to the floor on top of it. Talks to*
7 *Mother watching her.)*
8   **No one even spoke to me. No one sat with me at**
9 **lunch.** *(Beat)* **Yes, of course the teachers called my**
10 **name. They call everybody's name. One teacher didn't.**
11 **English. She had had some of the kids the year before,**
12 **so she'd just look up to see who was there.** *(Like the*
13 *teacher)* **"Hi Johnny, did you have a good summer? Oh**
14 **Suzanne, nice to see you again," a real big welcome.**
15 **The rest of us, she had to look at the list, and I got**
16 *(Sterner)* **"Musgrove? Sharon?" like it was some kind**
17 **of strange name she had never heard before. All day,**
18 **that's all it was, "Musgrove? Sharon? Oh there you**
19 **are." I wish we could move back home, Mom. I don't**
20 **want to go back there tomorrow.**
21   *(Beat)*
22   **No one was mean to me. No one was "anything" to**
23 **me. I had to ask where the rooms were and all. They**
24 **weren't as hard to find as I thought they were going to**
25 **be. And then I just followed everyone else to get to the**
26 **cafeteria.** *(Beat)* **I didn't see everything. I wasn't hungry.**
27 **I saw the yogurt, and that's what I got.** *(Beat)* **I just**
28 **sat there. At a table. Some kids sat down beside me,**
29 **but they didn't speak to me.** *(Beat)* **No! I didn't say**
30 **anything to them either.** *(Beat)* **I don't know! I guess**

1   because, because I didn't want to — there were
2   three of them! *(Beat)* Yeah, they were girls, they
3   could have spoken to me! Mom, can't I go back to
4   Rushton? I could live with Marion, her folks wouldn't
5   mind. I don't know anyone here! I hate it! *(Buries her*
6   *head in her lap.)* Hate it! Hate it ...
7   *(Beat)* Yeah, I remember Sally. *(Beat)* No, I didn't
8   see her today! Why in the world would she be here
9   in Claridge? *(Beat)* Yeah Mom, mark one for Claridge
10   High. Sally Smalley won't be here to give me grief.
11   That's one good thing. You need to think up about
12   a hundred more. I could pack some clothes for the
13   week, and Daddy could drive me down to Rushton
14   tonight, and—
15   *(Mother interrupts.)*
16   Okay, that's one more. It was nice not to have to
17   get up at six o'clock to catch the bus this morning.
18   *(Beat)* Marion has to get up earlier. Her road is the
19   first bus stop. *(Beat)* No, I wouldn't know everyone at
20   Rushton High, but I'd know some of them. There'd
21   be somebody for me to eat with at least. Do you
22   know how long lunch is if you're sitting there by
23   yourself? Forever! *(Beat)* I didn't look. There might
24   be! I didn't look! There's probably some freak no
25   one wants to sit with, or someone with b.o., or
26   some fat guy. *(Beat)* Oh I don't think so. *(Beat)* Well,
27   there might be somebody else new. I guess it kinda
28   makes sense. There's a lotta kids, I don't know how
29   many, but it is bigger than Rushton. And they have
30   French, did I tell you that? I can take French next
31   year. *(Picks up school badge, reads it.)* Claridge High
32   School. Well, at least Sally Smalley isn't here.
33
34
35

Exchange Student

1   *(JAN, 16, at office door of school counselor)*

2   Ms. Hampton? I'm Jan Frankel. I made an appoint-
3 ment with you yesterday. *(Comes in door, takes a seat.)*
4 Thank you for making time for me, it's not a real life
5 or death emergency I've got here, but it's a problem
6 I've got to get moving on right away, and I didn't know
7 anyone else I could turn to. I didn't want to talk to my
8 parents about it until I had all the answers, and I
9 thought if anyone could help me you could.

10   You know Brad Fisher. *(Beat)* Yes ... who doesn't?
11 Did you know he's my boyfriend? We've been together
12 three years last June 16th. *(Beat)* Two years. He's
13 exactly two years older than me, but our birthdays are
14 both in June, so we celebrate them together and kinda
15 forget the two-year difference. *(Beat)* Oh yes! He is on
16 top of the world right now. I mean, they're not only pay-
17 ing his tuition, picking up his food and all, but he'll be
18 getting a check every month too. For spending money!
19 Oh, he said yes immediately, right over the phone, he
20 didn't even wait to think about it. Didn't ask the coach
21 what he thought, none of that. He's really excited.

22   *(Beat, counselor asks question.)*

23   Well, I was hoping he'd go to school here, at the
24 university. He applied, but they were still kind of going
25 back and forth with him about it, and they weren't
26 talking any thing like the deal that _____ *(Enter name*
27 *of state university.)* gave him. *(Beat)* It's so far away. I'm
28 not ever going to get to see him. Not like, if he stayed
29 here.

30   I need you to help me find a high school near

1   *(Enter name of state university).* I've been
2 thinking about those exchange programs, you know
3 they're usually like to Switzerland or some place.
4 We could do that right here! Within the state! I
5 could go to a high school close to   *(Enter name*
6 *of university),* and someone from that school could
7 come here. Wouldn't that be neat? For the school
8 too! I mean, you could find out all sorts of stuff
9 about how they do things at other schools. And, if
10 you can find another girl for me to exchange with,
11 we could probably trade families too. She could
12 have my room and I could have hers. That way it
13 wouldn't cost anything either. And I've got a car. I
14 could even leave that here, for her, because, well,
15 you probably heard, Brad gets a car too, a new car!
16 It's all part of his scholarship. So, I wouldn't need,
17 well, I won't be hurting for a car if I'm with him.
18   No, I hadn't actually heard of anything like this,
19 but maybe you have a friend at that high school
20 near   *(Enter name of university)*? Or a friend
21 who knows a friend, another teacher or a counselor
22 or something, and you could call them up and
23 explain the situation. You'd be starting something
24 new! *(Beat)* I'm going to die here without Brad. I'm
25 not going to do well at all. And it's going to be a
26 hard enough year already, what with second-year
27 algebra and physics, and I just hate American
28 history. I know I'd do better if I didn't have to be
29 away from Brad too. He'd be on my mind all the
30 time! I just know it. I'll be sitting there in class and
31 I'll be thinking about him. I do it enough already!
32 But now, when I catch myself doing it, I look at my
33 watch, and I tell myself, you'll see him in twenty-
34 five minutes. Then I'm okay. I can wait a few
35 minutes. *(Beat)* But can't you see? I'll just die if I

1   have to tell myself twenty-five days! I'll just die!
2   *(Buries face in hands, then manages to recover.)*
3   **Can't you help me? Please?**
4
5
6
7
8
9
10
11
12
13
14
15
16
17
18
19
20
21
22
23
24
25
26
27
28
29
30
31
32
33
34
35

I'll Never Be Able to Look at Him Again

1   *(DOLLY, 16, inside a bathroom, talking to a friend on*
2   *other side of locked door. She has only in the last minute*
3   *stopped crying.)*
4   Uh-uh ... uh-uh ... No! Go away, Suzanne ... oh, no,
5   no don't, are you there? *(Beat)* Can you see him,
6   Suzanne? Can you see Jerry? *(Beat)* What's he doing?
7   *(Beat)* Betty?? He's dancing with Betty? Up close? How
8   close? Yeah yeah yeah, I feel a little better. There's
9   nothing left inside me. I'd kill for a Coke. No no! Don't
10 go. Stay and talk. I don't want people banging on the
11 door. Is he still dancing with her? Yeah, water, I've had
12 water. All the tap water I can drink. I look horrible. I
13 can't believe people are dancing again, you sure
14 they're not talking about me??
15 *(Beat)*
16 Betty ... Betty? I can't believe Betty made a move
17 on him. You think so? Did you see him ask her? He's
18 a jerk. He doesn't like her. He's never even noticed
19 her. I look horrible. I don't have my purse! I must've
20 left it in the car. Jerry's car. No, don't ask him. Let
21 him forget about me for awhile. Maybe if he dances
22 with enough other girls, he'll forget I threw up in front
23 of him.
24 *(Beat)*
25 He did? He cleaned it up? I'll never be able to look
26 at him again! *(A wail)* Oh Suzanne! I'm going to stay
27 in this bathroom forever! Until everyone else is gone. I
28 don't care how long it takes. I'll stay 'til morning. I'll
29 walk home.
30 *(Beat)*

1   This was my big chance with Jerry. Marlene just
2 happened to be out of town. He hadn't even heard
3 about the party until I told him. He asked me if I
4 was planning on going. If I wanted a ride.
5   *(Beat, a question, followed by a wailing answer)*
6   I don't know! We were dancing real fast, were
7 you watching us? I mean, I was going round and
8 round, I felt myself getting dizzy, but ... I mean, I've
9 been dizzy before and it hasn't made me throw up.
10 We were having such a good time! We had danced
11 to every song ... he's a fabulous dancer ... is he still
12 with Betty? No! don't tell me, I don't want to know.
13 *(Beat)*
14   No! I wasn't drinking! Where did you find any
15 booze at this party?? *(Beat)* Well, I didn't find any
16 either. I had a few slices of pepperoni pizza, then I
17 had some chips. I had some of the cheese stuff with
18 them. And a Coke. And some cake and some of the
19 chocolate chip cookies. Nothing out of the ordinary.
20 I wish everyone would just go home. Has anyone
21 left? Well, maybe you could go back out there and
22 start something. Turn down the music, and tell
23 Betty you just heard her parents drive up. I hope
24 Jerry won't be driving her home. I'm going to open
25 the door now. If he looks for me ... he won't ... *(She*
26 *opens door and sees Jerry standing just outside.)* Oh, hi
27 Jerry. You're not mad at me? You still like me? You
28 still want to dance? Okay. Let's dance!
29
30
31
32
33
34
35

Trophies

1   *(ANITA, 16, with girl friend, showing her jewelry)*
2   This is what I just got. It's not aquamarine — it's
3 the same color, but this is blue topaz, so it didn't cost
4 as much as it could have, even though it's a pretty big
5 stone. Aquamarine this size would cost four times as
6 much. Pretty, huh? And these are— *(Interrupted)* that's
7 right. Rubies and diamonds. Mom's borrowed these a
8 couple times already. She said she only had garnets
9 and pearls when she was sixteen. Oh well. Just goes
10 to show who's the smarter one, don't you think? But
11 I always let her borrow them. It makes her feel good.
12   What have you got? *(Beat)* You're kidding? It's easy
13 to get what you want. You just ask. Have you asked
14 them? *(Beat)* Oh, that's a line. They can all afford it,
15 they just say they can't. But they can always put it on
16 a credit card. Pay a little bit every month. It's not a big
17 deal, believe me. *(Beat)* Hmmm ... Well ...
18   Listen, I think you have got in some bad habits
19 with your parents, and if you like, I'm going to tell you
20 how I do it. Okay? Number one. Don't even introduce
21 the subject if they're in a bad mood. If you have
22 something you want, don't just come right out and
23 ask for it. Ease into it — ask them how their day went,
24 how they're feeling, how they slept, you get the
25 picture, that kind of thing, to see if the time is right.
26 This is very important right at the beginning, because
27 this is the first pitch, and if they get bad vibes, that's
28 what they're going to remember every time you bring
29 it up again.
30   Number two, always tell them straight out what

1 you want. You don't want any confusion — you don't
2 want them to find a cheaper model. This was the
3 very first thing I asked for, *(Holds out a charm*
4 *bracelet)* and let me tell you, you learn a lot with your
5 first request. These aren't the charms I wanted.
6 These are the charms I got. You see, I thought they
7 would buy me the bracelet and maybe one charm,
8 and then I would let them know which ones I wanted.
9 But they picked out a bracelet and had all these put
10 on it, right then and there. I learned two things with
11 this — they were willing to spend the money, and
12 they needed specific instruction. So, be sure to tell
13 them all the particulars, and let them know nothing
14 else will do. A picture's good. If you can show them
15 a picture, they can even carry that to the store.
16   Now if you find they are putting up a resistance,
17 put the pitch aside until a special kind of moment
18 arrives. I call it "the need to show their love"
19 moment. Like when you get a good grade they're
20 not expecting? Or right after you've spent a whole
21 bunch of time with them and they're feeling kind of
22 warm and fuzzy about you, "We're so proud of our
23 girl!," you know those times, well, make 'em pay off.
24 Have a request at the ready so they can really show
25 their love.
26   I don't know what I'm going for next. I'm getting a
27 little tired of jewelry. There's not a lot of opportunity
28 to wear it, but I like to look at it though, and show
29 people. You know, like some kids have their trophies
30 on a shelf, to show off all their accomplishments.
31 Well, I've got mine in a drawer. I tell you what I'm
32 thinking, though, what's been on my mind lately —
33 I've been thinking of a new red car. That white one's
34 just a hand-me-down. They didn't even have me in
35 mind when they bought it. *(Pulls out a large envelope.)*

1   They don't know anything about this yet. I've been
2   stopping by the dealers after school, picking up the
3   price sheets, looking over the cars. They'll be getting
4   me one. Yep, I'm going to have a brand-new car for
5   my senior year. Just you watch.
6
7
8
9
10
11
12
13
14
15
16
17
18
19
20
21
22
23
24
25
26
27
28
29
30
31
32
33
34
35

At Night on the Beach

1   *(DEBORAH, 16, driving, is just about to pull off the*
2 *road onto a beach. She brakes. The car stops, and she shifts*
3 *into "Park.")*
4   **This is beautiful! So beautiful. Not a soul around.**
5 **No one. It's heaven.** *(All of a sudden, uneasy. Checks*
6 *locks.)* **The doors are locked. Everything's okay.** *(Takes*
7 *hand off shift and turns off engine. Takes a deep breath and*
8 *sits back, relaxed.)* **It is so gorgeous here. Look at that**
9 **moon, going all white on the water. The trees, just**
10 **barely moving with the breeze.** *(Hears a birdcry.)*
11 **There's a little gull! Poor guy. Hasn't made it home yet**
12 **for the night. It is sooooo gorgeous.** *(A big sigh of*
13 *contentment, followed by a beat of silence. Then something*
14 *startles her.)* **What's that?** *(Looks all around.)* **Who's**
15 **there? Hello!** *(Listens.)* **Must've been something in the**
16 **water. A fish. A crab? They can be noisy. There's no**
17 **one here by you.** *(Relaxes again, breathing in this*
18 *wonderful scene.)* **You are such a big scaredy cat. Get**
19 **your license in June, and it takes until October before**
20 **you can get the nerve to stop on the beach at night?**
21 **And now you're ready to bolt? It's perfectly safe. It's**
22 **gorgeous!**
23   **So ... how about rolling the windows down? I'm**
24 **still scared? Of what?** *(Rolls her window down.)* **Ahhhh.**
25 **That's even better.** *(Breathes in the sea air.)* **It smells**
26 **wonderful!** *(Begins to hum a romantic tune, just reveling*
27 *in being there at night by herself — so delicious a feeling.*
28 *All of a sudden she really jumps up, frightened. Quickly*
29 *rolls up window.)* **Doors locked, locked? Yeah. Engine**
30 **on.** *(Turns it on.)* **Keep it on. You can go in a minute if**

1   the engine is on. *(Beat, she is very still, listening, her*
2   *heart pounding)* Don't hear a thing. Don't see a thing.
3   Someone could be down on the ground, though,
4   right by the car. Right outside this window. Right in
5   front of the wheels and I wouldn't see them. Why
6   Debbie? Why did you have to do this? There isn't a
7   single other person around if something happens to
8   you! This must be why they have that rule — No
9   One On The Beaches After Sunset. Not enough
10   people around to feel safe. How can a place so
11   gorgeous not be safe! *(Listens real hard.)* I'll put the
12   car in drive, and just let the wheels kind of move
13   forward, slow-like. Then if someone is out there,
14   they have a chance to run away before the tires roll
15   on them. *(Looks out the windshield.)* Oh yeah, real
16   smart idea. I end up rolling myself right into the
17   water. No. You have to back up. Gun the engine so
18   it will make it up the slope to the road. *(Looks out*
19   *side-view.)* Anyone hiding behind the car is sure to
20   get run over.
21   What is the matter with you? If someone is
22   there, they shouldn't be! Get outta here! Now! *(Pulls*
23   *transmission into reverse, and floors the accelerator.)*
24   Whoa! *(Brakes quickly.)* Look to see if there's a car
25   on the road, dodo, before you gun the engines at
26   fifty miles an hour. *(Looks all around and behind her.)*
27   Go! *(Hits accelerator pedal again, gets on road, makes a*
28   *turn, shifts into drive and is headed home.)* So, Miss
29   Scared, see anyone? Was anyone really there?
30   *(Looks into rear-view.)* Can't see. Can't really see.
31   Can't even see the boogey man, but that doesn't
32   mean he isn't there! *(Waves good-bye.)*
33
34
35

So Maybe I Went Too Far

1   *(MARSHA, 13, still a class clown, comes On-stage,*
2   *shaky, groaning. She's just been socked by Amy.)*
3   Ohhh ... ohhh ... I had no idea you could hit like
4   that. *(Touching her jaw)* Ooo ... ooo! I don't think I've
5   ever been hit right there. I remember falling on my
6   chin once. Face down, right to the sidewalk, when I
7   was trying to do that imitation of how Darin walks, you
8   know the one .... *(Starts a limping walk, almost falls*
9   *again.)* Whoops! *(Laughs.)* Marsha girl, you still can't
10 do it. And you don't need to go making this face of
11 yours any worse. Amy? Amy?? *(Looks around.)* I must
12 have really made Amy mad. Didn't even stick around
13 to see if I was hurt. *(Yelling)* Well, I am, Amy! You got
14 me good. *(Laughs.)* That ought to bring somebody.
15 *(Twinge of pain)* Ooooo! Better not open my mouth so
16 wide. Well, that's a bummer. *(Looks around.)* Wonder
17 where everyone went.
18   *(Long beat)*
19   You don't think, naaah, well ... ? Marsha girl,
20 maybe this time you went too far. Naaah, it was just
21 a joke. And besides, Amy's the one that started it. If
22 she didn't have her mouth open all the time, I would
23 have never come up with *(A fast finger thrust right to the*
24 *audience as if in Amy's face)* "Bzzzzzzz, here comes a
25 fly!" "Bzzzz, here's another one!" "Ooooop! Bzzzz,
26 just one more." *(Falls out laughing.)* The first time I did
27 that to her ... wow! She fell right back, knocked a
28 chair down, hit Bill Brader who was standing behind
29 the chair — a whole chain reaction just because she
30 had her mouth open.

1   *(Laughing so hard, has to catch herself when she*
2   *realizes her jaw is hurting)*
3   Stop it! Stop it, stop hurting. Why'd she have to
4   hit me? I thought she'd gotten used to me "doing
5   the fly." She didn't even fall down again. Not that I
6   saw. And everybody always thought it was funny.
7   Like the time I came at her from behind when we
8   were at the stadium. *(Does it with a curve.)* **Bzzz!**
9   Jumped right off the bench — I got her good. And
10   then there was that time at assembly, when I had
11   been up on stage, and came down to take my seat,
12   and there she was, sitting right there on the aisle,
13   mouth open ... *(A low finger thrust)* **Bzzz!** I really
14   surprised her that time. She was even watching me
15   walk back to my seat. And just as I passed her,
16   **Bzzz! Bzzz! Bzzz!**
17   *(Smiling, remembering her triumphant moment. Then*
18   *remembers something else that wipes the smile off her face.)*
19   She mumbled something to me that day, what
20   was it ... We were walking out of assembly, Amy
21   comes up to me from behind, and goes *(Mumbles*
22   *two words)*. That's what she said! The same thing
23   she called me today, "Half-brain!" *(Like Amy)* "Half-
24   brains shouldn't stir up trouble they aren't smart
25   enough to get out of." And that's when she socked
26   me. Everybody else must've heard that. *(Feels her*
27   *jaw.)* Hmmm ... it's getting bigger. I hope it's not
28   swelling up! What is it they tell you in first aid?
29   *(Beat)* Ice! Put ice on it right away! You knew that,
30   why are you standing around here? *(Hits hand to*
31   *head.)* Ow! *(Exasperated, walks away.)* Maybe Amy's
32   right, Marsha girl. *(Beat)* No, you're just hurt. Feeling
33   a little fuzzy. You're smarter than she is any day.
34   *(Finger thrust out)* **Bzzz!** *(Hits her jaw doing it.)* Ow!
35   *(Exits.)*

What Do You Mean By "Special"?

1   (MELISSA, 15, on opposite end of a couch from her
2   date, Roger, who has had his hands all over her just
3   before.)
4   No. You stay put. You stay right there. (Giggles.)
5   Until I figure this out. (He is inching over to her.) I tell
6   you what. I'm going to move over to that chair, and
7   you are going to stay on this couch. (Gets up, motions
8   to him to stay put.) Down. Down, boy! I am not trying
9   to tease you. I'm serious.
10   (One more move on Roger's part)
11   No! I'm important to me. (Giggles.) There's lots of
12 time. (Giggles.) My parents won't be back for hours.
13 Hou-ers. Now don't move. Back. Sit back down.
14 Thank you.
15   (Giggles.)
16   So. Special, huh? What do you mean, special?
17 (Motions him back down.) No! nothing more, not until
18 you answer the question. You said I was special, so
19 I'm asking you, what do you mean?
20   (Beat)
21   Oh yeah? Well, that's kinda funny 'cause that's
22 exactly what my parents say too. "Special is special."
23 Well, I think special is a peculiar word. I don't ever use
24 it. I'll tell someone they have fantastic eyes, or I would
25 kill for hair like theirs, or that they have a really gorgeous
26 figure, I spell out what ever it is about them that is spe-
27 cial. I would never just say "You're special." So,
28   (Giggles.)
29   Tell me what you think of me. Like, do you think
30 I'm pretty? (Beat) So, why didn't you say that in the

1   first place, instead of special?
2   *(Beat)*
3   Uh oh ... "Pretty in a special way" is a lot like
4   "special is special" ... You know, Roger, I really like
5   you, but you'd better come up with something
6   better than that if you think anything's going to
7   happen between us. So what's pretty about me?
8   *(Beat)* Well, am I pretty like Carol Tompkins? No,
9   forget it, I'll say it for you. No! No one's that pretty.
10   So, am I as pretty as Linda Fletcher ... or maybe
11   Ginger Rosti?
12   *(Beat)*
13   Oh Roger, this is not good. Special isn't good
14   enough anymore. Mom's been using it like forever.
15   I can't remember the first time I heard it, but it's
16   like, always been the answer whenever anybody
17   else was talked about as pretty, and I would ask her
18   if I was pretty too. That's always been her answer,
19   and I've never understood it other than ... other
20   than it was a way of saying I was not pretty. Even
21   Dad picked it up, he started saying it too, the exact
22   same nothing word. So I don't ask them that
23   question anymore, and I'm not going to ask you
24   that question anymore, but if you, sitting on that
25   couch over there, don't think there is something
26   attractive about me, I don't know why you are
27   hanging around! I'm not going to settle for some
28   kind of meaningless word. I'm waiting to hear
29   specifically what you like about me, or you can
30   leave, now.
31
32
33
34
35

Don't Make Me Yell at You

1   (ANNIE, 14, standing in front of mirror, about to try out
2 what she is going to say to her good friend, Ruth.)
3   The trick is, Annie-girl, to say "no," and still have
4 Ruth as a friend. So, you've got to sound not too hard,
5 but still hard enough to make her stop. (Beat) Funny.
6 I could try to make it sound funny. (Tries one.) "Oh
7 Ruth! You'll never believe what this new girl next to me
8 in history was trying to get me to do! I mean I don't
9 even know her, I mean I wouldn't even have spoken to
10 her if she wasn't sitting right beside me, and you know
11 what she asked me today? Listen to this! If I wanted
12 to go to her Sunday school next Sunday! She knows
13 nothing about me! Me! Who's been going to the same
14 church for fourteen years."
15   No. Ruth would ask a thousand questions about
16 the new girl. She wouldn't make the connection.
17 (Beat) There's always sincere. "Ruth, we've been
18 friends since third grade and you know I'd do anything
19 for you, I mean if you needed help with anything I'd be
20 there in a minute, but ..." Nope. She might get hung up
21 on something else, like the time I didn't come with her
22 to Girl Scout camp, and we'll never solve the problem
23 at hand. Nope — straight to the point, that's what it
24 will take.
25   So. The next time she asks me to go to Bible study
26 with her, because she will ask me, I could say, "You've
27 asked me before, remember? And I said no." And she'll
28 probably came back with, "Well, I thought you might
29 have changed your mind." No, the polite "No" doesn't
30 do it. I've tried that, she's going to keep asking until I

1 say something more.
2   So. I could say, "Why do you keep asking me
3 that?" Why does she do it? Maybe they make her.
4 Maybe they make everyone swear they'll bring a
5 friend next week. Well, if that's the deal, she's just
6 going to have to find another friend to go with her.
7 So I could say, "Do you need me to go with you for
8 some particular reason? You know I'd do anything
9 for you if you needed me, but I am really not
10 interested in going to your church."
11   "I'm really not interested in going to your
12 church." That doesn't sound so wonderful. She'd be
13 hurt. *(Beat)* Would I be mad if someone said that to
14 me? Hmmm ... hard question, but then I never ask
15 anyone to come to church with me. Not unless
16 there's a party or something. And that Bible study
17 of theirs is definitely not a party.
18   I could say, "Can't we be friends without going
19 to the same church? I don't insist you come with
20 me. In fact, you've never been to my church." And
21 she'd say, "That's because there's something going
22 on at my church every night of the week, and I know
23 you have Wednesday nights free." "Aaaggghhh!
24 Ruthie, don't make me yell at you! You've got to
25 understand I am not looking for another church!
26 Please, if you have to take someone with you, ask
27 someone else!" Well, that's pretty direct. *(Beat)*
28 'Course, I could always start my own Wednesday
29 night Bible study. Now there's an answer.
30
31
32
33
34
35

Part Two:
Monologs for Girls
(Serious)

Apologies

1   *(ROBIN, 14, about to knock at front door of house,*
2   *makes several false starts.)*
3   I can't do it, I can't do it, I can't do it. *(Covers face.)*
4   Oh I really screwed up this time. *(Takes time, finally*
5   *straightens up.)* I've got to do it. *(Puts hand up again to*
6   *knock.)* Maybe no one will be home. Shoot! what if
7   they are both home! *(Still hasn't knocked)* One would
8   be enough. If I can apologize to one of them, that
9   would be enough for Dad. *(Looks at watch.)* Four
10 o'clock. Missus Robbins might be fixing supper. She'd
11 be mad if I make her burn the chicken or something.
12 I'll come back later. *(Starts to go, stops.)* But then
13 Mister Robbins will be there too. It would be the two of
14 them. I'd rather apologize to just one. Mister Robbins
15 can be kind of funny. He might have even taken the
16 whole thing as funny. Except he's the one that had to
17 ... It wasn't funny. I know he wan't laughing. I'd kill
18 someone if they ran over Mussy. *(Shudders.)* Oooo! I
19 don't even want to think about it. And then they come
20 up to apologize to me? There's nothing they could say
21 — it'd be their fault, no matter what.
22   But I didn't mean to — it was an accident! I didn't
23 even see the cat. I don't remember seeing anything,
24 that's the real problem, and I know they're going to
25 ask me why didn't I see it. Then they're going to ask
26 me all the same questions Mom and Dad did. Why was
27 I in the truck in the first place? Didn't I know it's
28 illegal to be driving out in the street? Why did I have
29 to turn the engine on? What did I think I was doing?
30 Dad never seems to do anything without thinking

1   about it first. Mom remembers every single thing
2   that ever happened to her.
3   All I remember is, I was in the driver's seat, and
4   then all of a sudden, I backed out into the street. So
5   I switched gears to go forward. And the truck kinda
6   jumped, and then it stopped. And I got out. And ran
7   away from there as fast as I could. When I finally got
8   up my nerve to go home, Mom and Dad were sitting
9   on the porch. They asked me if I knew anything
10 about how the truck got out in the street. I told
11 them maybe the truck slipped into neutral and
12 rolled out by itself. We walked over to it, and there
13 were the keys still in the ignition and my purse on
14 the seat. They told me the Robbins' cat was found
15 under the front wheel.
16   That's the story. It doesn't sound very good.
17 Even telling it to myself. I don't remember turning
18 the key. I don't remember starting the engine. I
19 don't remember putting it in reverse. I do remember
20 looking around to be sure no one was watching before
21 I got in the truck. And I do remember switching gears
22 to go forward. It's that part in between. I must have
23 been pretty nervous. I can't believe I killed their cat.
24 I won't ever do anything like this again! Maybe
25 they'll believe that. I believe it.
26   *(Raises hand to knock again. Stops.)*
27   If I don't tell them, Dad will. And I'll be grounded
28 for two months instead of one. I did it. I'd better
29 just get on with it.
30   *(Finally knocks.)*
31
32
33
34
35

You Could Be Twenty-One, Too

1   (SUZY, 16, comes in, all excited, to show her best
2 friend, Annie, her latest triumph, a false i.d. that had just
3 arrived in the mail.)
4   I'm telling you, Annie, it was so simple! We walked
5 into this office, motor vehicles they called it, and my
6 cousin told them she was there because she didn't
7 drive, and she needed to get one of those identification
8 cards, so she could prove her age and all that. The
9 lady gave her this form and told her to bring it back
10 when she had filled it out. So we went over and sat
11 down, and she —(Beat, Annie interrupts.) Yeah, yeah,
12 yeah, you have to take something with you, she had
13 her birth certificate, that was plenty. So anyway, we
14 sat down, and she filled it out, but then, I, I signed her
15 name. Then, she took the form back, and the lady told
16 her to hold onto it and go stand in another line, to have
17 her picture taken. So I stood with her, just talking you
18 know, acting like we were just passing the time waiting,
19 and when her turn came up, I went up instead, and I
20 got my picture taken on her card. (Jumping up and
21 down, uncontainable) And here it is! That's me! See!
22 And it says I'm twenty-one. I'm twenty-one! And you
23 could be twenty-one, too! (Beat) They sent it to her
24 house, and she called me yesterday and told me to
25 come get it. (Beat) Naa, nobody else saw it.
26   (Beat)
27   Oh sure, she's got a regular drivers license, but it's
28 under her married name — not the one that shows on
29 her birth certificate. So now I can go anywhere I want,
30 buy anything I want, I can do anything I want! Can you

1   stand it?! I can't wait to go out to Black Jack's! I'm
2   going to have a margarita! I'm going to stay there
3   'til they close. I don't care who sees me, I have my
4   i.d. and I can do anything I want.
5   *(Joyous)*
6   Come on, come on Annie! who can we think of to
7   get one for you? I wish you had some older cousins here
8   in town, they're perfect, but, uh, you don't, so, uh ...
9   maybe there's someone at your church? *(Beat)* You
10 don't want one?! Are you out of your mind? Who
11 wouldn't want to be twenty-one? *(Beat)* Oh ... I am not
12 going to get in trouble! Nobody in those places really
13 cares how old you are. They just care about this little
14 card. *(Beat)* Come on, Annie, I don't really want to do
15 Black Jack's by myself. It'd be more fun if you went
16 too. *(Beat)* No one would see us — no one that would
17 tell anyway. *(Beat)* They go there?? I didn't know that.
18 My parents don't even know where Black Jack's is.
19 Well, it's not the only place in town, we can always go
20 somewhere else.
21   *(Beat)*
22   A crime? What kind of crime? I never heard that!
23 Who said it? Who told you that? *(Beat)* They won't
24 put you in jail for a little thing like this. Well, I don't
25 think my cousin would have done it if she knew it
26 was that illegal — *(Interrupts herself.)* You're just
27 jealous, Annie! You're jealous you didn't think of it
28 first. *(Waving the i.d.)* This is not going to get me in
29 trouble — it's going to set me free! *(On her way out)*
30 Bye! I'll tell you tomorrow what Black Jack's is li —
31 *(Interrupts herself)* well, maybe I'll go somewhere
32 else. I don't want to run into your parents my first
33 time out. *(Comes back.)* You ... you don't ... do you
34 really think I could be arrested? Just for having a
35 fake i.d.?

He's My Dog!

1   *(CHERIE, 13, at home, anxiously listening to her father*
2 *who is on the phone to the vet)*
3   **Daddy. Daddy ... What's he saying, tell me, tell me.**
4   *(Beat)*
5   **What's the matter, Daddy? Tell him just a minute**
6 *(As if yelling into a phone receiver)* **Hold on a minute,**
7 **Doctor Yankel! Daddy's got to tell me what you said!**
8   *(Beat)*
9   **He's gone, I know he's gone. Tell me, Daddy, isn't**
10 **he ... oh ...** *(Wail)* **Rusty!** *(Obviously distressed)* **Rus-ty!**
11 **You were the best dog we ever had!!! I love you, Rusty!**
12   *(When she recovers, looks over at Dad, now off the*
13 *phone.)*
14   **I guess Doctor Yankel was right ... I'm glad we took**
15 **him anyway. At least we tried.** *(Beat)* **And he probably**
16 **was not in so much pain either. I mean, he couldn't even**
17 **stand up anymore. He had to be really hurting.** *(Beat)*
18 **Yeah. That was good.** *(Beat)* **Can we go get him now?**
19   *(Beat)*
20   **What do you mean? Why would we —** *(Interrupted*
21 *by Dad)* **But I —** *(Interrupted again)* **Daddy! Daddy, call**
22 **him! Call him before he does something with him!**
23 *(Beat)* **We can bury him! I'll bury him!** *(Beat)* **I don't**
24 **care how long it takes to dig a hole. I'll do it! But call**
25 **Doctor Yankel before he does something with him!**
26 **He's my dog! I want him home! Please!** *(Beat, smiles, a*
27 *very slight smile through her distress.)* **Thank you.**
28   *(Turns away from Dad, while he is on phone.)*
29   **Oh Rusty.** *(Sits on the floor, imagines Rusty on the*
30 *floor with her.)* **You were the cutest little puppy I ever**

1 saw. You were so soft. You used to love to climb up
2 right here inside my knee. You'd stay there forever
3 if I let you.
4 *(To Dad, just putting down the phone)*
5 What'd he say? Can we go get him now? *(Beat)*
6 One hour, okay. I'll be here. I'll be right here waiting
7 to go. *(Beat)* I'm all right. *(Beat)* I know we tried.
8 Ready in an hour!
9 *(Dad walks away, CHERIE watches him, then again*
10 *imagines Rusty now grown with her.)*
11 Everyone said how pretty you were. Everyone
12 who saw you said what a pretty dog you have, what
13 a pretty face, what pretty eyes ... I loved you, Rusty.
14 When we get you home, I'll wrap your blanket
15 around you. I'll put your raggedy towel under your
16 chin. I don't know where we're going to put you ...
17 maybe back where you caught that mole. The
18 ground's pretty hard this time of year ... Daddy will
19 have to help me ... but I've just got to see you
20 again. Feel your ears. Your nose. Brush your hair.
21 You always liked for me to brush you. I'll go get your
22 brushes now. I'll wash them up, and they'll be all
23 dry by the time we bring you home. I'll make you
24 real pretty again.
25 *(Exits.)*
26
27
28
29
30
31
32
33
34
35

I Never Expected Anything Like This

1   *(Pretty CHRISTINE, 16, dressed up, stands with her*
2 *hands behind her back; something is in them, but we don't*
3 *see it.)*
4   I know a lot of you out there, watching me speak
5 in front of this large crowd, think I must be very sure
6 of myself. I'm not. I never expected to be here in front
7 of you. When I was younger, I was very shy. Mother
8 told me that when I was really small, just starting to
9 walk, I was not shy at all. She said I used to go right
10 up to people and start talking. Apparently, I would
11 always get their attention, and they would look at me,
12 but then they didn't hear what I was saying because I
13 was such a surprise to them. You see I was a very
14 strange-looking little girl. I had no hair. My eyes were
15 very pale. My teeth were bucktooth, which made my
16 smile kind of funny. And my face was short, you could
17 say squashed. Mother said people would turn away
18 from me. I made them uncomfortable. So, after a
19 while, and Mother has told me this too, I stopped
20 going up to people. I guess even at that age I realized
21 I was getting a bad reaction. And I became shy.
22   When I started off to first grade, Mother made a
23 point of telling me, and not just once because this I
24 do remember, that I was not ever going to get the
25 same attention that other girls got. But that she was
26 going to do everything she could to make me into a
27 talented person, and that I would have friends and do
28 just fine, but that I should not expect people to oooo
29 and aaahh over me. She said there was more to life
30 than being pretty.

1   So I was always the best student I could be, and
2 I learned to play the piano, and tennis, and learned
3 to cook and do pirouettes. And when I was old
4 enough, I got my teeth fixed, and went to modeling
5 school, and always had the best clothes Mother
6 could afford. Then all of a sudden, when I was
7 fifteen, my looks began to change. Even Mother was
8 surprised. And people began to treat me differently.
9 They began to smile at me more. They didn't turn
10 away as much as they had. But me, I was still shy.
11 That friendly little two-year-old had gone away a
12 long, long time ago. And people I met now, for the
13 first time, thought I was stuck-up, because I wasn't
14 always smiling, I wasn't as chatty as the other pretty
15 girls. I haven't quite learned how to be that, yet.
16   So, what I wanted to tell every person in the
17 audience, is that not all of us up here grew up think-
18 ing we are pretty. And no matter what we look like
19 today, we may still be those shy little ugly ducklings
20 underneath. *(Holds up trophy she's been holding.)*
21 Thank you, Mother. Thank you, judges. Thank you,
22 Chamber of Commerce. I can't tell you how honored
23 I feel to be Junior Miss Annapolis.
24
25
26
27
28
29
30
31
32
33
34   '
35

Going Home

1   *(MARTHA, age 14, is sitting on a curb with a quiet*
2 *friend.)*
3   *(Sighs.)* I really should go home. It's almost dark.
4 Pretty soon there won't be anyone even walking by.
5 Just the cars. With their headlights shining on me. I
6 hate having to decide where to go. It used to be so
7 easy. Home was one place — you knew where to go.
8 Why the hell did they have to get divorced?
9   Dad and I got in a fight last night. He told me to
10 go stay with Mom if I wasn't going to follow the rules
11 at his place. "No TV, no nothing unless the home-
12 work's done. Ten o'clock, lights off. No back talk. No
13 heavy makeup for school. No guys in the bedroom."
14 Sometimes I can't believe this is the one I like!
15   My mother will act very glad to see me. She'll give
16 me a big hug. Ask me to tell her everything that
17 happened in school. And after I've been talking, oh,
18 about two minutes, something in the kitchen will
19 catch her eye. "Keep talking" she'll say, "I'm just
20 going to. . . water the cactus." Whatever. Then she
21 will remember something that needs doing in the
22 kitchen, and then she'll forget I'm even there, and
23 then I can go back to my bedroom and get on the
24 phone, and have boys over, and go to sleep when I
25 want, and pick out whatever I want to wear to school
26 the next day. I won't see her again. In the morning
27 she'll knock on the door, "Martha? You up? I'll see you
28 later." She won't even wait for me to answer. And when
29 she gets to the bank, she'll brag to all her buddies that
30 Martha's come home to her momma. I hate her.

1   *(Sees a car coming.)*
2   **Uh-oh. Hey! Hey don't go!** *(Friend leaves.)* **Shoot.**
3   *(Car pulls up beside her.)*
4   **Uh-oh ...** *(Stands up slowly.)* **Hello officer.**
5   *(Rest of monolog should be interspersed with beats*
6   *as she is talking with the police officer.)*
7   **Me? Last night? Yeah, you know I think I did talk**
8   **to you last night. Yeah, I guess it was here on this**
9   **curb. Yeah, could have been about the same time.**
10   *(Laughs.)* **What do you mean doing business? We were**
11   **just sitting here, my friend and I were, well she had**
12   **to go home, but we were just talk —** *(Interrupted)* **I**
13   **don't know what that means. No! I don't want to go**
14   **with you to the station. Home? Well yeah, sure.**
15   *(Long beat before she gives address.)*
16   **Forty-four Woodway Drive! No I don't have an**
17   **i.d.,** *(Points)* **it's that way! I was headed there! Well**
18   **okay, I wasn't headed there yet, but —** *(Interrupted)*
19   **I am not a vagrant! I've got a home like everyone**
20   **else, Forty-four Woodway Drive, that's where my dad**
21   **is, that's where I was going as soon as I got through**
22   **with my friend. Yeah, I'm sure of it. I'd really rather**
23   **not, if you don't mind — I don't think my dad really**
24   **wants to see me driving up in a police car, I mean,**
25   **would you? Okay, I won't. Yeah, I promise. Tomorrow**
26   **you won't see me here. I'll be where I belong. Bye.**
27   *(Turns and walks away toward home.)*
28
29
30
31
32
33
34
35

Looking Pretty

1   *(SHERYL, 15, in front of a mirror, wearing a bulky*
2 *sweater. Actress should pick a color that looks fabulous on*
3 *her. Staring, particularly at her eyes)*
4   **Pretty eyes. Pretty eyes. Pretty eyes? I wonder**
5 **wonder wonder what he was talking about. I wonder if**
6 **I am ever going to know.**
7   *(Imitating her mother)*
8   **"You can't go out of the house again in that**
9 **sweater, young lady. Not until I have washed it."**
10   *(As if answering mother)*
11   **I'm not ever taking it off, Mo-ther!** *(Beat)* **I mean,**
12 **really, what if something happens to it? It could fade.**
13 **It could shrink. It could get caught on something, and**
14 **tear. And if I don't have this sweater on, he may not**
15 **recognize me. Ohh ... am I ever going to see him**
16 **again?**
17   **Wish I could figure out what in the world made him**
18 **speak to me. It was just Jeannie and me, sitting there,**
19 **in the booth by the window. I had my face in a soda.**
20 **So did she. But actually, we were watching people**
21 **come in. I saw him when he opened the door. Nice, oh**
22 **nice-looking. Dark shiny hair. Blue eyes. He looked at**
23 **me, I saw him! And he caught me staring at him! I**
24 **didn't dare look at him again. And then, all of a sudden,**
25 **there he was, standing beside us. He had on this light**
26 **blue shirt, the only one in the place. I kinda looked up,**
27 **and he said, "You have pretty eyes." And then he left,**
28 **just like that. "You have pretty eyes." I had never**
29 **seen him before. Jeannie didn't know who he was.**
30   *(Another long look in the mirror)*

1   All I can figure is, that I was wearing this
2 sweater. Lucky, lucky wonderful sweater. It covers
3 a lot. I mean, nothing up top, not yet anyway. Thick
4 waist, long neck. It's a good thing I was sitting
5 down, he couldn't see my flat rear. Big feet, long
6 legs. What if I'm taller than him! Oh please, no ... I
7 wish I were pretty. *(Beat)* He said I had pretty eyes.
8 I've been back to that same booth three days in a
9 row, but I haven't seen him again, not yet. I've had
10 this sweater on each and every time. I've worn it to
11 school every day.
12   *(Studies face.)*
13   It must be the sweater. My eyes aren't really
14 anything much. Hair? Somedays it isn't bad, but I
15 can't remember what it looked like that day. Lips,
16 hmmm, well, okay. Skin absolutely washed out! If I
17 hadn't put on makeup that day, he would never have
18 seen my eyes. Pretty eyes. "You have pretty eyes."
19   No one's ever told me that before. Daddy's always
20 saying, "You're frowning, Sheryl." Mother says, "Stop
21 squinting." If I told her what happened ... what? She'd
22 laugh. Then she'd say, oh I know exactly what she'd
23 say, "Are you sure he wasn't talking to Jeannie?"
24 They don't think I'm pretty. They never told me I
25 had pretty eyes.
26   It must have been the sweater. *(Yells out.)* I'm
27 not ever letting go of this sweater. *(Back to mirror)* I
28 don't care what she says.
29
30
31
32
33
34
35

I Don't Care if Nobody Likes Me

1   *(CHARELLE, 15, in her room at a juvenile detention*
2 *home. She is just writing the last sentence on a letter.)*
3   **Thanks ... for ... reading ... Charelle Andrus.** *(Looks*
4 *at letter, two pages or more, then writes.)* **P.S. Sorry ... it**
5 **... is ... so ... long ...** *(Folds pages and puts them into an*
6 *envelope. Just about to lick it and stops.)* **I'd better read**
7 **it over.** *(Takes it out.)* **Dear Missus Blakemore, Here I**
8 **am again. You said to write or call you anytime — I**
9 **hope you meant it.**
10   **I am writing to you because I can't use the phone**
11 **this month. Last week I got another month's solitary.**
12 **I am in my room by myself all the time. I don't get to**
13 **go to class. I do all the class assignments and take the**
14 **tests here in my room. Except for last week when all I**
15 **was allowed to do was think about why I do the things**
16 **I do that get me in trouble. This week I am supposed**
17 **to do this week's class work and last week's. They**
18 **don't know I'm writing to you. They will when they see**
19 **the envelope. Maybe they won't mail it. If they do, I**
20 **bet they'll read it first. Hi, Warden Spencer!**
21   **You probably want to know why I am in solitary**
22 **again. There was this fight. They said I started it, but**
23 **another girl did. She called me —** *(Picks up her pen and*
24 *crosses something out and writes this instead)* **some ...**
25 **bad ... things. I told her she'd better not ever do that**
26 **again, and she came right up in front of my face and**
27 **yell —** *(More cross out and writing)* **it ... again. So I hit**
28 **her. She fell down. Then all her friends took a punch**
29 **at me. I was down on the ground when the warden**
30 **finally got them off me. I don't know what happened**

1 to the others. I don't hear or see anything right now.
2   I hate this place. Nobody here likes me, but I
3 don't care. Nobody ever liked me. When you said
4 that I should write you, I didn't take it seriously.
5 Then you said I could call if I didn't want to write,
6 and that's when I thought maybe you meant it. I
7 thought maybe you like me a little. You remind me
8 of my mother.
9   All I want in life is to get out of here! I'm not
10 bad, not like some of these girls. I don't want to
11 hurt people. I don't want to steal other people's
12 stuff. I didn't know those kids were planning to
13 break into your house that night. I only knew one of
14 them, from school. I kinda had a crush on him, but
15 he'd never really noticed me before. When I left the
16 store, he was outside with the others. He called to
17 me, real friendly like. I couldn't believe he knew my
18 name. When he asked me if I wanted to ride with
19 them, I thought I'd died and gone to heaven. When
20 he asked me to drive, I didn't want to admit I was
21 only fifteen. I was afraid they'd leave without me.
22   You know all this. You heard it at the trial. I don't
23 know why I'm telling you again. I shouldn't have got
24 behind the steering wheel. I knew it was illegal — I
25 just didn't think it would lead to something worse. I
26 guess I don't have any other news, and my mother
27 doesn't want to hear from me. You don't have to
28 answer back. It's just kinda nice to know one person
29 is out there.
30
31
32
33
34
35

She's Always Doing That!

1   (MONICA, 14, at home with a brand-new friend, Amy.
2 Monica's mother has just left the room.)
3   **Thanks Mom, we'll call if we need you.** (Shuts door.)
4 **She's always doing that!** (Takes off hat she's had on.)
5 **She always has to say something cute about how I**
6 **look. And if I've got on something new, she doesn't**
7 **like it unless she picked it out.** (She has put hat on
8 another way.) **What do you think?** (Looks in mirror.)
9 **Hmmm ...** (Tries another way.) **I don't know. I think I**
10 **like it the way I had it on first.**
11   **She didn't like this either.** (The outfit she has on)
12 **First time she saw it, this boy, Jerry — oh! You'd like**
13 **him, I'll introduce you — he was here. I mean, it's bad**
14 **enough she embarrasses me in front of a girl she's**
15 **never met, but a guy? I kinda had this thing for Jerry**
16 **— he's real nice but he's not for me — so, but**
17 **anyway, I asked him to the Sadie Hawkins Dance —**
18 **that's a dance that's every year, it's great! Girls get to**
19 **invite the guys, but it's not 'til Spring — but anyway,**
20 **so Jerry came to the house to pick me up for the**
21 **dance. Mom didn't know what I was wearing. So Jerry**
22 **rings the bell, and she lets him in, and when I came**
23 **out, she says and I swear these are her exact words,**
24 **"I thought you were going to a dance. That looks like**
25 **something you'd wear to a funeral." I mean, is your**
26 **mom like that??**
27   **I was sooooo embarrassed! All I wanted to do was**
28 **grab Jerry and run out of the house, but I couldn't**
29 **move. I mean, I was stuck to the floor, I couldn't**
30 **move! And do you know what she did?** (Amy interrupts,

1   *MONICA laughs.)* **NO! No way! Your mom apologizes?**
2   **Not mine, no-ooo, she turned to Jerry and said "Do**
3   **you agree?" And he said, "I think Monica looks great."**
4   **He grabbed my hand, and he pulled me out the door,**
5   **and we ran for about a block until we realized we were**
6   **going the wrong direction, and then I fell on the**
7   **ground and so did he and we stayed there laughing**
8   **for the longest time. He's shorter than me now, but**
9   **he'll be just right for you.**
10   *(Beat)*
11   **Huh?** *(Amy repeats her question.)* **She's never said**
12   **another thing about it, and now I wear it all the time.**
13   **That's how she is. I don't mind her saying some-**
14   **thing, I mean everybody has a right to their own**
15   **opinion, but why does she have to say something**
16   **bad to me in front of somebody else? Why can't she**
17   **save it for when we're alone? Mom didn't know Jerry.**
18   **And, I mean, I just met you today, but that didn't**
19   **stop her, did it? No-ooo. She says anything to me,**
20   **any time at all, never mind how it makes me feel.**
21   *(Beat)*
22   **Oh yeah, she says some good stuff too, but I**
23   **don't think saying something nice gives her the**
24   **right to say the other stuff.** *(Beat)* **Let me tell you,**
25   **she's got herself into one bad habit.** *(Beat)* **Does**
26   **your mom do this too?** *(Beat)* **She's dead? Oh Amy!**
27   **A-my! why didn't you tell me? Why didn't you stop**
28   **me? I'm sorry. I'm, I'm so sorry, I didn't know, I ...**
29   **Was she sick? Was there some kind of accident or**
30   **something? You know, I'd just die if Mom left me**
31   **like that. I mean it's ... it's forever.**
32   *(Pulls hat down to hide her face.)*
33
34
35

It Could Be Me

1   (KAREN, 16, motioning to her mother that she doesn't
2 want to speak to the person calling her on the phone.
3 Listens to what Mom is saying, and motions to her hang
4 up. She finally does. To Mom)
5   Thank you. Thank you! I'll speak to her next time.
6 (Beat) I know she sounds bad, she did last time she
7 called, but ... I spoke to her then! I did! I did, and I
8 could swear it was just last week, don't you remem-
9 ber? Maybe you weren't around. I spoke with her the
10 whole five minutes. She told me she couldn't eat the
11 food, and she didn't have anyone to talk to, or any
12 music to listen to, and the place smelled bad all the
13 time. And, oh yeah, that she really missed riding
14 around with me. That she only got to go outside every
15 other day, in the middle of the afternoon, for only
16 fifteen minutes. But not if it was raining so one week
17 she didn't get outside at all. (Beat) Gee Mom, if you'd
18 just let the phone ring, we wouldn't even be having
19 this problem. I wasn't going to answer it. I knew it was
20 Nancy! She gets to make her call at the same time
21 each week — she told me that too, last week. (Beat)
22 Well, I can't help it. She made a bad choice, she
23 should have called someone else. I wasn't her only
24 friend, you know!
25   (Beat)
26   Yeah? Well, maybe you should be like some of the
27 other mothers, maybe it's not such a great idea for me
28 to keep up with someone in prison. (Beat) I don't
29 know! I just didn't feel like talking to her right this
30 minute. (Beat) No, I'm not saying she stopped being

1 my best friend, but it's not exactly the same thing,
2 I mean, she's not around. She's not at school, I
3 can't just call her anytime to talk, we're not even
4 doing the same stuff anymore, and besides ...
5 *(Beat)*
6 Well yeah, it is a real downer to talk with Nancy
7 now. *(Beat)* I do sympathize with her situation! If
8 cheering her up was all there was to it, I would've
9 been waiting for her call. I would have had her
10 favorite songs playing, so she could hear 'em for at
11 least five minutes a week. But you know what? Even
12 if I had played them for her, she wouldn't hear
13 them. She would talk the whole time, and I just
14 don't want to hear it! I don't want to hear about the
15 rats and the smells and how dirty it is ... it could be
16 me there! I could have been in prison, too ...
17 *(A quietness comes over her.)*
18 That night Nancy got caught, they came by here
19 to get me. I was going to go with them. We were
20 going to tag along wherever the boys were going. She
21 didn't know what they had planned. I didn't either.
22 But I had a stomachache, and I thought it might get
23 worse, so I didn't go. Going along on a armed
24 robbery, and we didn't even know it? Accessory to a
25 crime? I could be there too, Mom, I could be in
26 prison too! *(Beat)* Every time Nancy calls, that's
27 what goes through my mind. That's why I'm not
28 dying to talk to her.
29
30
31
32
33
34
35

Making Up

1   *(CARMEN, 17, in girls' bathroom at school. Looking into*
2 *mirror, while pulling on her make-up, starting with base*
3 *foundation. She is speaking to someone who came in.)*
4   When I was real little, I actually thought people
5 couldn't see me. I would be out on the playground,
6 and the other kids would run right past me without
7 ever slowing down, without ever saying, "Come on,
8 come on and play with us!" *(Beat)* Mama likes to say
9 "Just a touch of color, that's all you need." *(Laughs.)*
10 Puh-lease!
11   *(Adding shading to her cheeks)*
12   Shading is important. My cheeks are round, but
13 the shading takes care of that. You can do anything
14 with it — straighten your nose, shorten your chin,
15 widen your eyes — it's like, *(Laughs)* some sort of
16 magic! *(Applying rouge)* I love rouge. The real thing,
17 not that powdered stuff. It goes on way too light.
18 Rouge is the only thing Mama will wear. She uses it
19 on her lips too. I don't know why she bothers at all.
20 *(Using a long pencil on her brows)* I don't want those itty
21 bitty brows — *(Makes a heavy arch)* oh yeah, there it is,
22 a good strong line. By the time I was in seventh grade,
23 I had a big revelation. No boys were hanging around
24 me — not even the ones the other girls turned down.
25 And one day, I realized that the boys were treating me
26 like people did my mama.
27   I had watched her a thousand times from our
28 window, before I was even old enough to go to school.
29 She would go out every day — still does — to get food
30 for supper. She would let me stay home if I stood in

1   the window where she could see me. You can see all
2   the way to the store from our third-floor window. I
3   would lean way out just to see her come out the
4   front door. Then she'd walk down the steps, one,
5   two, three — five steps, and then turn into the
6   street. There were people everywhere, and she'd be
7   walking among them. *(Proudly)* There goes my
8   mama! I'd say out loud. But you know, no one ever
9   stopped to speak. No one ever turned their head. I
10   think I was the only one who saw her. One day when
11   I was in seventh grade, I was home, sick. When she
12   went out, I stood at the window again, watching her.
13   And that very day I vowed not to go through life like
14   that. *(Working on eyes)* These eyes are my biggest
15   problem.They'd just fade away if I left them alone.
16   Mascara takes a lot of time. You want to get as
17   much on as those little hairs will hold, but not so
18   much that it gets inside.
19   *(Beat)*
20   I get most of my ideas from magazines. I must
21   have looked at hundreds of pictures and finally
22   came up with a face that stops 'em cold. Mama
23   doesn't like this at all, so I get to school about this
24   time every morning. No one else is usually around,
25   it's awfully early, but I have time to do it right. Red
26   lipstick's the best. It always stands out. I put it on,
27   then blot it ... dust powder over that ... then I do a
28   second coat. The powder kind of seals it on. *(We
29   hardly recognize the person we met at the beginning.)*
30   This will only last me a couple hours, but let me tell
31   you, the boys do look at me.
32
33
34
35

The Twelve-Hour Car

1   *(SALLY, 16, at home pacing up and down)*
2   Think, Sally, think. What to do. What to do. Can't
3 call. Can't call anyone! Phones — locked in Dad's bed-
4 room. Can't leave the house. *(Imitating her dad)* "It'd
5 better be a damned certain emergency for you to take
6 one step out of this house, young lady." Fire. I could
7 set a fire. That'd show him. *(Beat)* I'd never get my car
8 back then. I'd probably end up in jail. What is going
9 on here! I'm probably the only kid in history that had
10 a car for just twelve hours. Twelve hours. There must
11 be others, but they probably wrecked their cars. Me?
12 My car looks perfect, but I get it taken away.
13   *(Hears something.)*
14   What's that?
15   *(Goes to window, looks out, raises it.)*
16   Hi Amy! How'd you know I was here? No, it's not
17 broken, it's been ringing and ringing. Dad's locked all
18 the phones and the TVs and even the stereo controls
19 in his bedroom. No, I don't have the key. Yeah,
20 grounded again. No, I can't let anyone in. And if you
21 hear a car, beat it. I'm not supposed to be talking to
22 anyone.
23   *(Beat)*
24   I wasn't drunk! *(Beat)* Who told you that? I'd just
25 had a sip, a little sip, that's all. You know my dad
26 usually has a drink at night, but last night, for some
27 reason, he hadn't had a drop, so he could really smell
28 just that little bit on my breath. I don't know what
29 made Dad go out last night. And he wasn't in his car,
30 he was in a company truck, so I didn't notice him

1 when I pulled in at the gas station. I didn't even see
2 him until I went inside to pay, and he yells out
3 "Sally!" So I said hello, and Dad says, "Come give
4 me another birthday hug," so I gave him one of
5 these guys *(Cheek kisses)*, and he says, "I think I
6 deserve a bigger greeting that that" which is when
7 he smelled the beer. Then he looked out the window
8 and saw everyone in the car, and he says "I thought
9 I said no one in the car until you get real familiar
10 with it. Didn't I just give it to you this morning?"
11   *(Beat)*
12   Oh yeah, he was mad. He said, "Take all your
13 friends back to their own homes, and then you
14 come straight to the house." So here I am. Going
15 on the second day. How drunk could I have been if
16 he told me to drive them home first? He was mad
17 that I had anyone in the car with me.
18   *(Beat)*
19   I don't know where the car is. Not here. He said,
20 "I am impounding it until you and I come to an
21 understanding." Sure, I'll get it back. He always
22 softens up, you just don't know how long it will
23 take before he does. *(Beat)* **Naaa ... he never caught**
24 **me drinking before.** *(Beat)* **Yeah, I know, drinking**
25 **and driving ... Believe me, I heard it all yesterday a**
26 **million times.** *(Beat)* **Yeah I know kids get killed, but**
27 **I know how to drive, I've been driving for years.**
28 **Whose side are you on anyway?** *(Beat)* **Really? All of**
29 **them? They've been grounded too? Just for being in**
30 **the car with me?** *(Beat)* **Well, listen, tell 'em for me**
31 **that as soon as I can think of a way out of this, I'll**
32 **come get them, and this time you too, and we'll do**
33 **it again.** *(Beat)* **Oh really? Well, be that way, Amy!**
34 **Maybe that's why I didn't pick you up in the first**
35 **place!** *(Slams window.)*

Second Chances

1   *(HELEN, 17, in a school bathroom, talking to the girl in*
2 *the next toilet stall)*
3   **Hello?** *(Knocks on wall.)* **Hello? I know you're there.**
4 **You didn't think anyone else was in here, did you? You**
5 **don't have to answer. You and your friend started talking**
6 **the minute you came in, and, well, I heard everything.**
7 **I know you're upset — that's probably why you didn't**
8 **check real good to see if anybody else was here.**
9 **Listen, I'm not going anywhere, and I don't want to**
10 **embarrass you, but please, don't go yet. You don't**
11 **know me, and you sure weren't expecting to get**
12 **another opinion, but I'm going to tell you what I think**
13 **anyway, which is, "Tell your parents."** *(Hears girl open-*
14 *ing stall door, HELEN stands up.)* **Wait! Wait! Don't go!**
15 **I'll run after you and see who you are! I will tell your**
16 **parents! I would! I would!** *(Beat)* **Thanks. Thanks for**
17 **staying. You know, another opinion isn't such a bad**
18 **idea. The one you got already, the one I heard, that**
19 **was a friend talking. She uh, she might've been**
20 **saying what you wanted to hear.**
21   **So, I say "tell your parents" because if something**
22 **happens during the ... the procedure, or maybe after-**
23 **wards, some sort of complication or mistake or**
24 **something, then the whole thing won't come as such**
25 **a shock to them. I mean, it will be bad enough for**
26 **them if you get hurt, they'll have to deal with that**
27 **which won't be great, but it would be even worse if you**
28 **got hurt and, by the way, they lost a grandchild, too.**
29   *(Girl comments.)*
30   **Yeah, they might try to stop you. But hey — you**

1 can always find a way, I mean, if that's still what
2 you really want to do.
3   You know what you've got is not the end of the
4 world — I mean, from their point of view. It's not as
5 if you're on dope, or as if you were dying, or as if
6 you were paralyzed from a car crash or something.
7 Having a baby is not so out of the ordinary, it's not
8 something they won't be able to understand. And
9 you know, and I have a feeling from what you told
10 your friend that this idea may not have occurred to
11 you, but, your parents might just want the baby. I
12 mean, it's not just your baby, it's theirs too. They
13 might want the chance to raise it themselves. I
14 think you should at least ask them.
15 *(Long beat)*
16 Do you hear me? Hello? *(Gets a minimum*
17 *response.)* Thanks. I was beginning to think you put
18 a roll of toilet paper in your ears. Listen, I ... I did
19 what you're thinking of doing. It, uh, it was no snap.
20 And, uh, it was about a year ago, and, uh, I still
21 think about it. I think about the baby. I think, how
22 old would the baby be now? *(Beat)* I didn't tell my
23 folks. No one even suggested it to me. But I know,
24 now, that they would have wanted it. They would
25 have raised it as theirs. Things would have been
26 just fine. I really wish someone had told me what
27 I'm telling you. And uh ... *(Beat)* there's just one
28 more thing. I've had some problems since then. I
29 mean, everything went all right at the time, but I've
30 had problems since then. I've seen doctors — it's
31 nothing they can't treat, but they have told me not
32 to expect a baby next time just because I want one.
33 Thing is, you don't always get a second chance.
34
35

Coming Into Heaven

1   *(WINONA, 15, lying down, eyes closed, groans softly.*
2 *All of a sudden there is a change in the space around her,*
3 *which stirs her.)*
4   **Huh?** *(Raises herself up on elbows, stares straight*
5 *ahead.)* **What's that? Such a bright light ... bright ...**
6 **bright ... oh my ... oh my gosh ... Oh no ...** *(Awestruck)*
7 **Oh no!** *(Beat)* **I can't be. I can't be dead!** *(Looking out,*
8 *searching)* **Is anyone there? Hello?** *(Shielding her eyes)*
9 **It's just like the books say, a bright bright light and**
10 **nothing else. You feel yourself being pulled by the light**
11 **and it becomes brighter and brighter ... Heaven.**
12 **Coming into heaven. But nobody ever says what**
13 **happens after that.** *(Pinches herself.)* **I felt that! The**
14 **books say your body feels light, light as air, that you**
15 **feel as if you are floating and you see your body lying**
16 **below you. I don't feel that way. I'm not floating. I**
17 **hurt!** *(With a cry of anguish)* **Where am I?**
18   *(Falls back, lying on floor again. Finally moves a foot.*
19 *Then the other. Then her arms, and then when she puts*
20 *them back down, she feels something else.)*
21   **Sheets? I don't think I'm in heaven. Oh, I hurt!**
22 *(Takes a big breath.)* **I'm breathing.** *(Sings out.)* **Aaaahh!**
23 **I can hear myself. Where am I?** *(Yells.)* **Is there nobody**
24 **around here?**
25   *(Beat)*
26   **Last thing I remember was ...** *(Feels what she is*
27 *wearing)* **shorts ... shorts! Running, I was running on**
28 **the field ... I was feeling sick, but running, running**
29 **anyway. Miss Switzer keeps saying, "Get the lead out,**
30 **Winona, get the lead out, what's the matter with you**

1   today, what'd you have for lunch? Something fried?
2   you're way behind time, way behind ... "
3   *(Beat)*
4   I must have fainted. I should have told her. I
5   should have told her what happened in math class.
6   The nurse having to come there to see me. I wish
7   the nurse had sent me home. She did send me
8   home ... but I wouldn't go. I'll go home when the
9   bell rings, that's what I told her, and then I went out
10 to the track instead. *(Looks around her.)* **Winona, you**
11 **are in an ambulance. You are somewhere. You are**
12 **stopped. Someone must have opened the doors.**
13 **They must have gone for help.**
14   *(Raises up again, and yells.)*
15   Isn't anyone there? *(Beat)* **You are so stupid,**
16 **Winona. Why didn't you tell Miss Switzer? Trying to**
17 **impress the coach? That's what you were doing.**
18 **Push yourself. Don't admit weakness. And where**
19 **did it get you? In an ambulance? Aaaagghhh ...**
20   *(Her groan followed by long beat)*
21   I must have fainted. I remember pushing, pushing,
22 trying to make one foot hit the ground, then the
23 other, feeling as if I'm not even going forward, not
24 even moving, just pushing, feeling my knee come
25 up and my foot hit the ground, light-headed ... oh, I
26 think I am going to, going to ... faint ... again ...
27   *(Voice trails off, collapses.)*
28
29
30
31
32
33
34
35

Part Three:
Monologs
for Guys
(Humorous)

First Job

Jamming

It's Awfully. . . Frilly in Here

I Got to Meet Olajuwon!

The Lesson

Dancin' Fool

Karate Klutz

Stock Boy

Outside Door

Throw Me the Ones You Don't Want

The Con

Hang Ups

What Am I Thinking About?

First Job

1   (MARK PETERS, 18, wiping down tables in a fast food
2 place, and talking to another young employee)
3   No one I know ever comes in here. Two weeks ago I
4 wouldn't even have come into a place like this. I didn't
5 grow up wiping down counters and cleaning up toilets.
6 I never even had a job before this. When school got
7 out, I could do whatever I wanted. Watch a movie,
8 hang out, drive around ... This is the first "job" I've
9 ever had. If I have to work, I should be in an office.
10   My dad, he knows people. So does Mom. Both of
11 them! I don't know about your parents, but mine didn't
12 even try to get me something better! You know what
13 they pulled on me? You know why I'm here? We were
14 eating dinner one night, nothing special going on, and
15 out of nowhere Dad says, "Mark, now that you gradu-
16 ated, we're not paying for anything other than the loan
17 on your car. You're going to have to support yourself
18 one day, so you might as well get started now." All of
19 a sudden, it's on me — the insurance, the gas, the oil,
20 repairs! Everything!
21   No, they're still making the payment. Big deal.
22 They expect me to pay for everything else. (As his dad)
23 "If you don't get a job pretty soon, that car won't be
24 able to move out of the driveway." He made this big
25 thing of "filling me up with one last tank of gas."
26   I asked them to talk to their friends about giving
27 me a job, and you know what they came back with?
28 "You can call any of them you want." So when the car
29 ran out of gas, I started walking. There was a Help
30 Wanted sign in this window. That was my first day at

1 work. Gerry paid me a few bucks up front, so I could
2 go get my car.
3   They came by the other day, my parents. Both
4 of them. I thought they had come to say they were
5 sorry, that I didn't really have to work here, but no,
6 they acted real proud of me. Proud to see me in a
7 place like this?! And, listen, listen to this. Now
8 they're saying they're not going to pay for college
9 either.
10   *(As dad)*
11   "If you go to school here in town, it won't cost
12 you much at all. You'll be able to cover all your
13 expenses with this job."
14   I'm not living with them any longer. Moving out
15 as soon as I can. But do you know how much money
16 it takes for an apartment?! I went out looking, that
17 same day they came in to see me. I'll never make
18 enough. Not working here.
19   You know, my life was just fine, and now, now,
20 with all these changes, I don't know what's happening
21 any more. It could be just something my Dad is
22 going through. It doesn't sound like Mom. Some-
23 thing could be going on between them that has
24 nothing to do with me, that's what Jason, you know
25 Jason Taylor? Well, that's what he keeps telling me
26 anyway. He says if I just give them some time, they
27 might change their minds. That's what he tried with
28 his parents last time he got into it with them. And they
29 came back around. 'Course, he didn't have to spend
30 time working in a place like this. I don't know how long
31 I can take it. This ain't me. No sir. This is not me.
32
33
34
35

Jamming

1   *(BILL, age 15, comes out, playing guitar, but we don't*
2 *hear a sound. He goes at it something wicked, sometimes*
3 *singing out.)*
4   I love to play. Sorry you can't hear it, but my dad
5 makes me unplug after ten o'clock. That's when I have
6 to do my French. Can you tell what I'm playing? Just by
7 watching me? I'm kidding you, it's an unfair question.
8 You wouldn't know it 'cause I'm just goofing off.
9 Playing my own thing. *(Hums a riff for us.)* It's different
10 every time. What I'm dying for is one of those computer
11 programs that prints out what you're playing. Then I'd
12 have copies, on paper, of exactly what I'm hearing now,
13 and even other people could play my stuff. Everyone
14 says I'm pretty fantastic on guitar, I mean, I'm not
15 trying to brag, it's just my thing. You know how that
16 goes. I'd like to be in a band but ... not until ... The deal
17 here, is, I can't be in a band until my French grade
18 improves. Mom and Dad, they want a "B."
19   I hate French. It's not that I can't do it, it's that I
20 don't like doing it. You have to work at it. You have to
21 sit with all this stuff — the book, the paper, the
22 pencil, a little dictionary, and then you have to con-
23 centrate. You can't, well, I can't even have any music
24 playing because French is so boring that any little
25 distraction will suck your mind right off the page. And
26 then you have to memorize all these words, all these
27 verbs, all this grammar that has nothing to do with
28 anything! And pretty soon you find yourself with the
29 guitar in your hand, trying not to make a single little
30 sound that would give you away. Can't let dad know

1   what I'm doing.

2   I tried to get out of it, but the school has this

3   language requirement. I don't have a problem with

4   any of the other subjects — I mean I read 'em, I get

5   'em, math, history, all that stuff comes easy — not

6   as easy as the guitar, but not a wrench either. Not

7   like French. *(Beat)* A wrench, that French — hey,

8   maybe I can use that.

9   Dad says I've been lucky, that everything before

10   this has come too easy. He says, "French is a test,

11   a test of your ability to apply yourself." What does

12   he think I am doing when I am playing music?

13   "Goofing off." That's what he calls it. But look, I

14   say, if when I goof off I am brilliant, why would I

15   want to struggle and only come up average? Am I

16   missing something here? They want a "B!"

17   *(Starts to sing syllables to what he is playing.)*

18   "A be, a be, a be be be be be. Je suis a be, a be"

19   *(Stops)*

20   Je suis? How'd that get in there? *(Sings again.)*

21   "Je suis a be, une francais a be, je suis a be, je suis,

22   attendez, a be." *(Takes a look at plug.)* Put the French

23   to music? Now this might be something even Dad

24   might like to hear. *(Plugs in.)* Dad. Hey Dad! *(Leaves,*

25   *singing.)* "Je suis, a be, attendez, a be ... "

26

27

28

29

30

31

32

33

34

35

It's Awfully . . . Frilly in Here

1   *(EDDIE, 13, standing at the door to his older sister's*
2 *bedroom. Sleeping bag in hand. Can't bring himself to step*
3 *inside)*
4   Hey. Yeah, here I am. You look busy, I mean, I know
5 I promised to come, and, I mean, here I am, but, gee
6 Sis if you need to do something — *(Beat, she interrupts.)*
7 Yeah, I know it's a good night. *(Beat)* It's not that I don't
8 want to spend some time with you ... but ... what do
9 you think about doing this in the den? You can have the
10 couch, I can drag the bag anywh — *(Beat, she interrupts.)*
11 Yeah, well, that's true enough. But hey, we could pull
12 out a mattress for you, that's no big deal — *(Beat, she*
13 *interrupts.)* Yeah, that's true, no door. You think we're
14 going to be that loud? I mean, I though we were just
15 going to talk — *(Beat)* Yeah, you're right, they'd be
16 suspicious. Mom would listen.
17   *(Beat)*
18   I'm coming in, I'm coming in, I mean, aren't I here
19 already? I'm just, just, how do you stand all this? All
20 this ... fabric stuff everywhere?? *(A real visceral reaction*
21 *to the overdone frilliness.)* I don't see where I can put my
22 bag down that I won't be lying under some of it, and,
23 I mean, I know you like it or you wouldn't have filled
24 up the room with it, but I'm not real comfortable with
25 a lot of ... lacy stuff! On me. *(Beat)* Haven't you
26 noticed I ... I haven't been in here? Not since Mom let
27 you redecorate? I mean, I know you can't stand the
28 way my room is always so messed up, but this, this
29 gives me the creeps. *(Beat)* Maybe it's some kind of
30 guy/girl thing. Maybe all guys have a hard time in

1 rooms like this. I mean, I think this bro/sis night,
2 this idea of yours is great, and, hey look, I even
3 picked up candy bars for us, but ...
4 *(Puts the sleeping bag down, unrolls it.)*
5 I'll just put it down here in the doorway a while. Take
6 a little time to see if I can get used to being in here.
7 *(Sits stiffly on bag, allows himself to look around.)*
8 **Geez! How do you stand it!** *(Listens to her, laughs.)*
9 **Good move! Good move. Don't ever invite him in**
10 **here! It would scare him away.** *(Shudders.)* **I like**
11 **Tom. He's not bad. One of your better choices.**
12 **Yeah. Stick to the den. Or the kitchen. Don't risk**
13 **bringing him in here.** *(Looks around again.)* **Although ...**
14 *(An inspiring idea hits him.)* **Naah.** *(Beat)* **Well, I was**
15 **just thinking, your girlfriends really like this too, don't**
16 **they. I mean, I know they sleep over.** *(Beat)* **Well,**
17 **maybe, maybe if I could get used to it, maybe after a**
18 **couple of these bro and sis nights, like you were**
19 **saying, every Thursday or something, maybe then**
20 **that girl I was telling you about** — *(Beat, interrupted)*
21 **That's right, Janet, maybe if she comes over to**
22 **study or something, we could** — *(Beat)* **Yeah! Study**
23 **in here! Some night when you've got plans. To be**
24 **out.** *(Beat, Sis asks a question.)* **I guess I am. A little.**
25 *(Gets up, pulls his bag inside a little further. Lies down*
26 *this time, then Sis says something.)* **Huh? Oh. Yeah.**
27 *(Gets up, closes the door. His bag is right beside it. Lies*
28 *down again. Looks up at the canopy above her bed.)*
29 **I really don't like that thing over the bed. You can't**
30 **see the stars and planets on the ceiling anymore. I**
31 **used to sneak in here when you spent the night out.**
32 **Before all this got put in. I'd lie on your old bed, and**
33 **look up at your sky. I'd pretend you were here too.**
34 **We'd talk about all sorts of things.** *(Beat)* **Yeah.**
35 **Kinda like we're doing now.**

I Got to Meet Olajuwon!

1   *(ABE, 14, still high from the thrill of his lifetime, spots a*
2 *friend. Note: feel free to replace "Olajuwon" with another name*
3 *that equates supertall basketball star to your audience.)*
4   Hey! Jimbo! you shoulda gone with me! I met
5 Olajuwon! Yeah. Yesterday. At the game, man. I'm
6 telling you, it was fantastic, you shoulda gone, you
7 shoulda gone. I mean, you know me, all I ever wanted
8 to do was meet Olajuwon, and I've done it, man, I've
9 done it! *(High five or some similar show of glee)*
10   I didn't even think we were going to get inside the
11 game. I mean, free tickets? It sounded like some sort
12 of joke. Yeah. I know. I thought that's why you didn't go.
13 Well, I said, what else you got to do this afternoon, Abe?
14 Take a chance. I figured if nothing else, I might see him
15 drive up or something. I got there early, I walked all
16 around, went by every door. Someone yelled at me, "You
17 lost, kid?" I showed him my ticket, and he said "Second
18 door on the left." I was so surprised, I mean, that I was
19 even getting in, and then I heard myself saying to this
20 guy, is there any way to meet Olajuwon?
21   He looked at me, he looked at me hard, then he
22 laughed, and said, "Well, not before the game, kid.
23 But, if it looks like they're going to win, go on down,
24 before the game is over, and stand outside the locker
25 room door. They'll be feeling pretty good after a win,
26 and ... well, you never know."
27   So I went down there, like the guy told me, and I
28 was just standing there, outside the locker room, I
29 mean I was excited just to be standing there! I could
30 hear the last couple of minutes of the game, and then

1   the whole team, every single one of the them came
2   running up to the door! They were all around me,
3   like I was one of them, and the door opened, and
4   Olajuwon pushed me inside! Yeah! The locker room!
5   And they were all yelling and joking and
6   hollering. Someone took a picture — I'll get it, I'll
7   get it — it was some guy from the paper, and he
8   took my name, and he gave me his number, said to
9   call him in a few days. Yeah, a picture of me. With
10   the whole team. And I'm standing right next to
11   Olajuwon! He asked me if I played. If I was any
12   good. Sure, I told him, sure I was good. Olajuwon!
13   *(Reliving the excitement)* **Olajuwon was talking to me!**
14   *(Lets himself go, enjoying the moment.)* **You shoulda**
15   **gone to the game, man, you shoulda gone.**
16   *(His pent-up energy spent, he is calm.)*
17   The thing is, and I wouldn't believe it if anyone
18   told me, but, after I'd been with him five minutes or
19   so, yeah, in the locker room, while he was getting
20   dressed, I gotta tell you — it was no big thing. I
21   mean, he's just a guy, like you or me, he didn't
22   even seem all that tall. Seven feet tall, I hear you,
23   and he looks huge on the court, but up close, he's
24   not all that big. It's kind of funny ... And after the
25   game, in the locker room, they're all just like us.
26   They talk about the same stuff. They look like us.
27   Even Olajuwon — he's just a guy.
28
29
30
31
32
33
34
35

The Lesson

1   (JEFF, 18, is in a small plane, sitting, with his legs
2 spread waiting in a line of about ten people to go out the
3 back of the plane. It is his first sky-dive. He is hooked to
4 instructor in front of him, to whom he is talking.)
5   I wanted to jump ever since I saw that movie, can't
6 remember the name of it, no, not that one. Flying
7 Elvises! They'll do anything to get attention. No, this
8 movie had all these people jumping out a plane, one
9 after another, boom, boom, boom, and they joined
10 hands as they fell, and formed a circle, and down they
11 went, just so, well, like they were floating, and I said I
12 gotta do It, I gotta do It, I gotta know what it's like to
13 float on the wind. So here I am. (Plane hits an air bump,
14 he reacts, someone asks a question.) Me? Nah, I'm not
15 scared. You scared? (Beat) Well, sure, that's right, we
16 wouldn't be here if we were scared. I'm just not used
17 to flying, not in a little plane like this. (Another bump,
18 reaction) They weren't joking about really feeling the
19 bumps in these cloud hoppers. (Head feels a little light.)
20 Whoa! You didn't feel that? (Reprise, not as bad) Not as
21 big a plane, so not as much weight, you'll get bumped
22 around a lot on the way up, yeah, yeah I remember.
23   (Feels his straps, checks them again, tight.)
24   Hey! Anybody's parents give you a bad time about
25 doing this? (Beat) Yeah, mine too. Same thing. Same
26 stuff. Absolutely. And did you get all the stories about
27 chutes not opening? (Beat) Oh man, I don't know
28 where they get these stories. I mean, what's a chute
29 for, except to open? That's what they're designed for,
30 right? That's what I told them, there's no reason these

71

1 things exist except to open on cue! Your mom tell
2 you you might forget to pull the toggle to open it?
3 Mine loved that excuse. *(Imitating her)* "You'll fall out
4 of that plane and be looking around, forget about
5 what you're supposed to be doing, and then you'll
6 hit the ground and we'll never see you again." Well
7 this arrangement put an end to that! Strapped to
8 the instructor? What could she say? *(Imitating her*
9 *again)* "How do you know he will pull the toggle? Is
10 he responsible? Do you even know him? Do you
11 even talk to him before getting into the plane?"
12   *(Beat, instructor says something, Jeff responds to him.)*
13   Yes sir, I checked my belt again. We're attached.
14 Tight. Have you even seen a chute that hasn't
15 opened? Really? Huh. *(Beat)* No, no ... I'm not scared,
16 I'm sure this one will open. *(Beat)* Just about there?
17 *(Looks around.)* Really? *(Air pocket jolt)* Whoops! Maybe
18 we shouldn't go first. Oh yeah, you're right, there's
19 not enough room in here to go to the back of the line.
20 *(Beat)* No, I'm not losing my nerve, but ...
21   *(Door opens, bottom slides up, disappearing into top*
22 *of plane, JEFF watches it, then looks out, almost falls,*
23 *catches top of plane with two hands.)*
24   Whoa! *(Instructor says something.)* No, I'm ready,
25 I just, I ...
26   *(Having problem getting enough air, it is thinner,*
27 *finally takes big breath)*
28   Yeah, I remember, the air's thin. And cold! Yeah,
29 you said it would be cold. *(Looks down, little dizzy.)*
30 Wow! It's a long way down. *(Instructor says something.)*
31 Ready? You're ready already? Did you check those
32 hooks? All four? Let go? Oh yeah, *(Removes hands*
33 *from door)* Cross my arms, yeah okay, *(Instructor from*
34 *behind pushes him)*
35   Aaaggghhh ... *(Falls.)*

Dancin' Fool

1   (CARL, 17, comes On-stage dancing, and humming his
2 own accompaniment, something like "Stepping out with
3 my baby," something dramatic with a bit of a storyline,
4 and we see he obviously loves dancing. Stops mid-step,
5 person watching him has stopped him.)
6   **Huh?**
7   (He listens to what the person is saying, then)
8   **Twist, turn, back step, fast stop? Sure, I can do it.**
9 **I can do any step anyone shows me, but let me see ...**
10 (Does the sequence.)
11   **That what you want? Or better yet maybe —**
12 (Not waiting for a reply, does it again with an extra
13 spin and quick stop. Person applauds.)
14 **Well thanks.**
15 (Beat, laughs.)
16   **It's not my life, no, you've got it all wrong. I enjoy**
17 **it. I always like to dance, but when is this show of**
18 **yours, exactly? I mean, I don't know if I can fit it into**
19 **my schedule.**
20 (Person remarks.)
21   **No, like I said, I'd like to do it, uh, I just have other**
22 **things to do, you know? School, there's always**
23 **school. Does this job pay?**
24 (Person remarks.)
25   **Just asking ... after all, you called me.**
26 (Does a tricky step, as if punctuating what he just
27 said.)
28   **Thanks, you're right — it's an original. An idea I got**
29 **last night that I was trying to work out before I forgot**
30 **it. Know what I mean?**

1   *(Beat)*

2   Huh? You don't dance? Really? Why not?

3   *(Beat)*

4   Even if I had no ability at all, I would still dance.

5   I mean, you don't have to want to be a chorus boy

6   to enjoy moving about. But still, chorus boy isn't

7   exactly what I'm aiming for. Any leads in this show?

8   You know, speaking parts?

9   *(Beat)*

10   Anything that would be good for me?

11   *(Beat)*

12   Already? You're kidding! I don't remember seeing

13   any other audition notices you put out. Was there

14   something in the paper?

15   *(Beat)*

16   Well, that's the way it is then.

17   *(Starts dancing something fast — breaks abruptly.)*

18   What'd you say?

19   *(Beat)*

20   Two weeks? Rehearsals start in two weeks? Any

21   bit parts? A line? Something more than just a

22   member of the chorus?

23   *(Beat)*

24   Well, I tell you what. I'll think about it.

25   *(Dances again — something wonderful — something*

26   *where we can see he can solo. We get the idea the person*

27   *is asking him to leave, but CARL keeps indicating "just*

28   *a second more." Finally he winds down.)*

29   Whew! That felt good. That's the reason I dance!

30   *(Starts to leave, then turns back)*

31   I almost forgot! I'll be in your chorus, if I don't

32   get a better offer before rehearsals start. Take it or

33   leave it!

34   *(Exits with a wave.)*

35

Karate Klutz

1   *(ROGER, 16, comes out book in hand, reading, and*
2   *trips over his own feet while walking out. ROGER is no*
3   *nerd or dummy, but he has been "all legs and awkward"*
4   *for some time now.)*
5   "Beginning position, the horse stance. Feet apart,
6   knees bent. Upper body erect with fists, palms up, at
7   the sides of the body." *(Puts book down to try.)* Feet
8   apart. Knees bent. Upper body erect. Fists, Palms up,
9   at sides of waist.
10   *(Leans over to look at picture, and falls.)*
11   It's not as bad as it looks, Roger. If this had been
12   a class, you might not have hit the floor. Think about
13   it. You fell when you bent over to check the book. You
14   wouldn't have had to check the book in a class. In a
15   class, the instructor would have come around and
16   said, that's it, Roger, you've got it. *(Picks himself up.)*
17   So, not bad for a first time out. I say, good show, keep
18   going. *(Tries again.)* Feet apart, knees bent, upper body
19   erect, fists at sides. The guy in the picture had his
20   chest kinda out, too. Wow! Feels good. Roger, you
21   just may have found the solution. A-ii!
22   *(With a yell, thrusts his left leg and left fist forward at*
23   *the same time, which throws him off-balance, and he falls.)*
24   Just have to try not to kill myself while learning it.
25   *(Looks at book.)* "Before extending the fist, take a wide
26   front foot position for good balance." Ah-ha! *(Gets up*
27   *to assume the stance again.)* Feet. Knees. Upper body
28   erect. Fists at side. Now, left foot front. Okay. A-ii!
29   *(Thrusts left fist forward, body follows, falls again.)*
30   Roger, you have been God's clumsiest animal for

1 three years now, and you still are! If this were a
2 class, they would be laughing, howling, carrying on
3 something fierce like they always do. *(As his unseen*
4 *classmates)* "The idea is to stay on your feet, Rog." "I
5 want Rog for my boxing partner — he falls without
6 you even having to come near him!" Maybe you did
7 something wrong, again. *(Picks up book.)* **Wide foot**
8 **position. The right fist is drawn back, the left is**
9 **then ... then, the left is then extended.** *(Stands up.)*
10 **Feet, knees, body, fists side, left foot front, right fist**
11 **back, A-ii!** *(Thrusts his left fist forward, and manages to*
12 *hold it.)* **A-ii!** *(Beat)* **Wow! Again!**
13   *(Retreats fists and legs back to original stance, then*
14 *tries it again, this time raising his left fist high in the air*
15 *instead of just forward.)*
16   **Foot front. Fist back. A-ii!**
17   *(He is overjoyed at his ability to just stand upright in*
18 *such a forceful position.)*
19   **You've got it, Roger, you've got it!** *(Moves back to*
20 *initial stance to do it one more time.)* **The punch,** *(Fist*
21 *straight out)* **A-ii!** *(Initial stance again)* **The guard,** *(Fist*
22 *out and up)* **A-ii! The slash blow.** *(Initial stance, then*
23 *a one/two slash/blow)* **A-iii!**
24   *(Falls down.)*
25   **And that, Roger, was too much of a good thing.**
26 **Remember why you are doing this in the first place?**
27 **Not to be the karate champ, but to keep from falling**
28 **over your own two feet all the time!**
29   **Save the funny stuff for class.**
30   *(Opens book.)*
31   **All right. "Basic foot and body coordination is**
32 **achieved by mastering the ... "**
33   *(Reading, walks away.)*
34
35

Stock Boy

1   *(DARREN, 15, at a grocery where he works stocking*
2 *shelves, taking a minute to talk to an attractive female*
3 *customer)*
4   **I get a fifteen minute break, coming up pretty soon**
5 **now, maybe just,** *(Has to look at his watch, something he*
6 *now does a lot for the first time in his life)* **looka there,**
7 **just a half an hour away. I could meet you over at the**
8 **deli, and we could sit and talk, or we could get some-**
9 **thing to drink and go outside —**
10   *(Beat, she interrupts, he checks his watch.)*
11   **Just twenty-nine minutes away now. You could,**
12 **uh, go look at the magazines, we got all the stuff**
13 **women like, or, uh, we got a pretty good cosmetics**
14 **aisle, I see a lot of girls hanging out there.**
15   *(She walks away, he goes after her.)*
16   **Hey, hey! Now why are you going without telling**
17 **me where you're going to be in** *(Checks watch)* **twenty-**
18 **eight, almost twenty-seven minutes?** *(Beat)* **You can't?**
19 **Even for me? Then, how about this? I get off work at**
20 **eight. I have to be home at eight-thirty, but there's a**
21 **half hour, twice as much time as a break, that we**
22 **could get together. Walking home, at night, in the dark**
23 **— don't you live down Richard Street? I could go that**
24 **way too.** *(Beat)* **Even better — you could drive me**
25 **home! And we could sit outside for a long while.** *(Beat)*
26 **I still have to go in by eight-thirty. Varsity rule: "In bed**
27 **by ten. Up at six for morning practice. Eight hours**
28 **sleep or don't bother to come." Three hours of home-**
29 **work has to get squeezed in between eight-thirty and**
30 **and ten.** *(Beat)* **I got the same schedule Monday**

1   through Thursday, Friday there's usually a game, so I
2   don't come to work on Fridays. Saturday and Sunday,
3   I put in eight hours here, five hours practice, eight
4   hours sleep, which leaves eight, thirteen, twenty-
5   one, leaves three hours a day for getting back and
6   forth and doing homework, and uh, oh yeah, going
7   to church on Sunday.
8   *(Beat, she's walking away again.)*
9   Hey, hey! I do have time for a girlfriend! I got
10   these three hours, and all these half-hours and a
11   whole bunch of little breaks, I got all sorts of time,
12   it's just got to be scheduled, you know what I
13   mean? You go to church? You haven't got a church?
14   *(Beat)* **Well,** see, there's a whole lot of time we could
15   be together. You could go to church with me, you'd
16   love it. They do all this singing, and the people are
17   real friendly, and everybody dresses up. I bet you've
18   got some great clothes you never get a chance to
19   wear. My sister does. She's always complaining
20   about never having enough places to go. And hey!
21   She goes to church. You'll already know somebody
22   else there besides me.
23   *(Spots a manager.)*
24   Uh, look, uh, twenty minutes, the deli? Bye!
25   *(Manager speaks to him.)*
26   Yes sir. She wanted to know, uh, if we had
27   pickles anywhere else in the store. Those ones we
28   got here, they weren't exactly the kind she was
29   looking for. I told her there might be some at the deli.
30   *(Beat)* **Yes sir. Courtesy Desk. I'll remember that.**
31
32
33
34
35

Outside Door

1   *(READE, 13, in his new bedroom at night with Scotty,*
2 *a friend who came into the house through the bedroom's*
3 *outside entrance.)*
4   Hey, come on, come on yourself! I'm getting ready,
5 don't you see me looking for my shoes? I'm moving on
6 it, I'm moving, we'll be out of here in a minute. And
7 keep your voice down, huh? They're on the other side
8 of the house, but still, I haven't been in this room long
9 enough to figure out what exactly they can hear. I know
10 they went to bed, the door's closed, but I don't think
11 they're anywhere near asleep. And you know how
12 sometimes, sometimes you can hear people talking
13 through the vents? Yeah I'm serious! It happens all the
14 time in this house. They'll be in another room, and I'll
15 hear 'em through the vent. Sometimes it's just the TV
16 *(Cocks an ear.)* I haven't really heard anything yet. Not
17 in here. Maybe I'll be lucky, since this is an addition,
18 maybe it won't be connected up like all the other
19 rooms are. I don't know, I'm still testing it. And by the
20 way, next time you come, don't knock so loud. Or
21 maybe you could call right before you come, and I
22 could leave the door open. No, forget that. I'll leave the
23 door unlocked whenever I'm in here. So when you
24 come, try the knob, and if the door is locked, figure
25 I'm not here. *(Beat)* Yeah, it's pretty neat all right.
26 *(Beat)* It wasn't even my idea. They said they were
27 tired of all my friends tracking dirt thought the den,
28 and they were going to put an outside door on my new
29 room, for them!
30   Is it cold out? I was freezing when I got in from

1   school! I am hurrying! I don't know where my jackets
2   are, some of that stuff is still in my old room. *(Beat)*
3   I am not stalling! Didn't I let you in? They told me
4   not to let anyone in after ten on a school night, so
5   don't talk about stalling. *(Beat)* I am not afraid to go
6   out! We're going. Aren't we going? How was I
7   supposed to know you'd come around tonight? This
8   is my first night in here. *(Beat)* So what'd ya think?
9   It's bigger, yeah, we don't have to sit so close to the
10   TV anymore. I still want a waterbed, but they're
11   putting me off. I'll probably have to get a job so I
12   can buy it myself.
13   *(Jacket and boots on)*
14   So. Where we going? *(Beat)* I thought you said we
15   had plans. I don't want to go anywhere. Who are we
16   meeting? *(Beat)* There's nobody else? What are we
17   planning on doing? Taking a walk?
18   *(Beat)*
19   Scot-ty!
20   *(Throwing his jacket off)*
21   It ain't worth it.
22   *(Looks around his new room.)*
23   It's gotta be something worth it if I'm going to
24   get in trouble. I know my mom. She's going to come
25   down to see me before she turns in, just to be sure
26   I'm all right. *(Like Mom would say)* "All the way over
27   there." That's what she's been saying all the time
28   this was going up — "Aren't you going to be scared
29   all the way over here all by yourself?" She'll come to
30   see how I'm doing, and if I'm A.W.O.L. the first
31   night on my own, I could lose this. I could be back
32   in my old room in a flash. *(Beat)* I got pizza. You
33   hungry?
34
35

Throw Me the Ones You Don't Want

1   *(ADAM, 14, good-looking, walking along the hall with*
2 *a friend, Tom. A girl passes, says hello to ADAM. To the girl,*
3 *as he walks on)*
4   **Hello to you too.**
5   *(Has to turn to answer her question, but doesn't break*
6 *stride.)*
7   **Sure, I'll be there. See you.** *(Beat, listening to Tom)*
8 **You got some imagination, Tom. Susan's just friendly,**
9 **she's not interested in me.** *(Beat)* **I didn't know she**
10 **knew you.** *(Beat)* **Algebra? When was that? Oh yeah,**
11 **we were all in algebra together, was it last year?**
12 **Maybe she didn't recognize you.** *(Beat, looks at Tom.)*
13 **You get new glasses since then?**
14   *(Another girl passes, says hello to ADAM.)*
15   **Hey to you too, Martha!** *(To Tom)* **You don't know**
16 **Martha?** *(Beat, listening)* **It wouldn't hurt you to say**
17 **hello, you could have said hello —** *(Tom interrupts.)* **Oh,**
18 **you're wrong —** *(Interrupted by girl passing who says*
19 *hello)* **Eileen! I didn't see you, hi!** *(Beat)* **I was talking**
20 **to you, I didn't see her.** *(Beat)* **What?? You're out of**
21 **your head, Tom, they're just being friendly, I don't**
22 **know why they're not speaking to you, but —** *(Girl*
23 *passing speaks to ADAM.)* **Hey! How ya doing?** *(To Tom)*
24 **Let's turn here.** *(Go in restroom.)*
25   **Now, what's all this about** *(Beat, Tom spits it out.)*
26 **Throw you the ones I don't want!** *(Laughs.)* **How about**
27 **speaking up for yourself!** *(Beat)* **They are not falling all**
28 **over me! They're just being friendly, and if you were a**
29 **little friendly, they would be smiling at you too. Throw**
30 **you the ones I don't want! Take 'em, buddy! Take 'em**

1   yourself! Aren't we walking along together? Aren't I
2   giving you enough of a start? I'm practically putting
3   them in your lap! You could've turned right around
4   and followed Martha. She would have spoken to
5   you. But let me tell you, if I called her and said she
6   ought to go out with you, it makes you sound weak.
7   Like you couldn't speak up for yourself. Now a blind
8   date, that might be something else, but who do I
9   know that you don't know too? Every girl who
10   passed us, you knew 'em. They could be thinking
11   that you're ignoring them. That you think you're too
12   good for them. That ever pass your mind?
13   Listen buddy, you and I have been hanging
14   together since first grade. I've been helping you ...
15   forever. You've been taking my scraps ... forever.
16   You got your drafting badge in scouts with drawings
17   from my trash. You took my fifth-grade science fair
18   project and turned it into a geography paper. You
19   even wear the sneakers I grow out of. And hey, I'm
20   not complaining. I'm a waste-not/want-not person
21   as much as anyone. But with girls, Tom, with
22   women, I'm telling you, you're out of line. They're
23   not scraps.
24   *(Beat)*
25   Just treat 'em like you'd like to be treated. Be
26   friendly. Nice. You'll get one on your own. *(Beat)* I
27   promise you.
28
29
30
31
32
33
34
35

The Con

1   *(SMITTY, 15, in his room, standing in front of a mirror,*
2 *trying out various alibis for his parents, as well as how he*
3 *looks while saying them)*
4   "Hey Mom, Dad, come on ..." *(Beat)* "Mom. Dad."
5 That's better. "I didn't even know there was a party! I
6 don't now why, but I just don't get in on as much as
7 you guys think I do. I don't hear everything. *(Beat)* Sure,
8 I still see Joey, but he didn't tell me he was having a
9 party last night. *(Beat)* Algebra, yeah, that's the class
10 we got together. *(Beat)* I don't know, I guess he was
11 there. I was paying attention to Mrs. Vander. I didn't
12 really look around to see who all was in class. Integers,
13 she was explaining integers again, and you know I've
14 always had a problem with them, so I was listening.
15 *(Beat, anticipating parents' probable response)* Yeah. For
16 once. You guys don't think I do anything right, do you?
17 But I tell you, I don't know if he was there. *(Beat)* Yeah,
18 she'd called roll, but I just sit there waiting for my
19 name, I'm not listening for anyone else's."
20   *(Breaks his pose, turns away from the mirror.)*
21   Nope, that's not going to fly, Smitty. Someone
22 may have already told their parents I was at the party,
23 and if that gets back to mine, I'm dead in the water.
24 *(Beat)* How about ...
25   *(Obviously looking into the mirror again)*
26   "Well, of course, I was there. Joey's still a friend of
27 mine, you know that." Hold it Smitty, that's coming
28 on way too strong ... *(While trying a couple other facial*
29 *expressions in front of mirror)*
30   "Yeah, I was there. Ye-ah, I was there. You're right,

1 I was there." That's good. "You're right, I was there,
2 everyone was, but I didn't realize Joey's parent
3 weren't around. *(Beat)* And I did that! I asked Joey
4 who was here and he said his dad was, and he was
5 in the john and would be out in a minute if I wanted
6 to see him. And I guess that's when some girl came
7 up to me, and we started dancing, and I just kinda
8 forgot to find Mr. Stryker after that." Not bad, that
9 might fly. What could they do to it? Nobody will
10 believe Joey if he tells them that the party was my
11 idea. 'Course they might ask why I didn't leave
12 when I smelled smoke. *(Beat)* You were outside,
13 Smitty! You were outside. With a girl? No, they'll
14 ask who. "I just went outside" Doesn't sound very
15 convincing. Why would I leave the action? *(Beat)*
16 Had to go! Somebody was in both bathrooms and I
17 had to go. Not wonderful, but Dad would relate. So
18 I'm outside, by myself, taking a leak, *(To mirror)* "I
19 didn't know anyone was lighting up inside. I saw a
20 police car pull up out front, and I went back in,
21 thinking, you know, someone might be hurt. And
22 that's how I got hauled in."
23   Yeah, that'll do it. *("Thumbs up" to himself in the*
24 *mirror.)* All you gotta come up with is something
25 they can't prove otherwise. And then hold to it.
26 Hold your ground. And don't go changing this story
27 midstream — that's what got you in trouble the last
28 time.
29
30
31
32
33
34
35

84

Hang Ups

1   *(WILL, 15, comes out, holding phone, in middle of*
2 *conversation, listening; his friend Dwayne with him.)*
3   Uh huh ... Huh huh ... No, no I'm still here. Yeah.
4 I said I was. Uh huh ... huhhhh. Well, I got to go —
5 Huh ... I've got ...
6   *(Getting more and more exasperated)*
7   Listen Jolie, I've got someone here, I really got to go.
8   *(Beat)*
9   I can't promise that. I'll see you tomorrow. Geometry!
10   *(Slams phone into his hand.)*
11   I'm going to stop answering the phone! Or get the
12 number changed. Or get my own line. But that'll cost
13 me ... I can't believe she doesn't have anyone else
14 to call!
15   *(Beat, friend comments.)*
16   Hey! Don't worry, we'll get 'em, we'll get those
17 answers. That test isn't due for two days, and Jolie
18 always comes through. When'd she fail us, huh? Tell
19 me, huh?
20   I wasn't mean to her! You sound like my mother.
21 The girl was cool. She understood having a friend over
22 and not wanting to hang on the phone. *(Beat)* What'd
23 she ask? She asked if I was going to call her back
24 after you left. Believe me, I'm not talking to her again
25 today. I'll see her tomorrow. We'll get those answers.
26   *(Beat)*
27   No way! If you're so worried about her, here's the
28 phone. *(Beat)* Believe me, she isn't picky about who
29 she talks to!
30   *(Beat)*

1   No, I didn't tell her I was passing you the
2 answers too. You know, I wish she'd asked me who
3 was here. I wouldn't have told her you! I would've
4 told her Marilyn was here. That would have put her
5 in her place. That would have shut her up. That's
6 the answer, you know. If I had a girlfriend already,
7 Jolie would do her bit, and then be outta my face. I
8 mean, look, that dame you get to help us in
9 physics? Does she ever bother you at home?
10   *(Beat)*
11   Yeah, well, a call or two I could handle, but look-
12 it! Jolie has even shown up here at the house.
13 Doorbell rings, I run 'cause I think it's some kind of
14 special delivery or something, but no, it's Jolie,
15 staring at me behind the screen door. *(Girl's voice)*
16 "Hi Will. What are you doing?" Minding my own
17 business, how about you? Slam!
18   *(Beat)*
19   Mom heard that one. Told me I was rude to her.
20 Made me go after her and apologize.
21   *(Beat)*
22   Hey! Believe me, Jolie will deliver the answers.
23 Have I ever been wrong on this before? Haven't I
24 been keeping you afloat all semester?
25   *(Beat)*
26   That wasn't bad, I tell you, and even if it was, I
27 am not about to call her back and apologize again.
28 That will definitely give the wrong message.
29   *(Beat)*
30   No way!
31   *(Beat)*
32   You wouldn't dare! Going to Dallas was my idea!
33 The guys would never go without me! Oh come on!
34 No! Come on ...
35   *(Voice trails off, a stand-off, finally he dials.)*

1   Hi! Jolie! Yeah, it's Will. Yeah, he's gone. Oh,
2   just some guy. Dwayne. Yeah, well, a bunch of us
3   guys are going to Dallas Saturday. Yeah, he'll be
4   driving. He's got the best car for the trip. So, uh, we
5   were just making plans and all. So what were you
6   saying before I had to hang up? Oh yeah? Uh-huh ...
7   huh ...
8
9
10
11
12
13
14
15
16
17
18
19
20
21
22
23
24
25
26
27
28
29
30
31
32
33
34
35

What Am I Thinking About?

1   *(BRAD, 15, sitting at a chair/desk in class. His math*
2   *teacher has just asked him, "What are you thinking*
3   *about?" He managed to answer something suitable, and*
4   *now his mind is racing.)*
5   Whoa lady, why did you ask me that? And how did
6   I ever come up with such a smart answer as subjective
7   conjunctions?
8   *(As his young attractive female teacher)*
9   "What are you thinking about, Mr. Bradley Fuster?
10   Can you share it with the rest of the class?"
11   *(As himself again)*
12   "Subjective conjunctions, Miss Malton. You're
13   right, I wasn't thinking about geometry. I'll get right to
14   it though."
15   *(Beat, then as if to the teacher)*
16   I'll bet you could tell exactly what was on my mind,
17   Miss Malton. Miss Molly Malton. Miss Molly Malton
18   Mighty Mathematician. Mighty sexy mathematician.
19   How can you think about isosceles triangles looking
20   like that? Walk over to this side, yeah, yeah, a little
21   further, hmmm! You are the best-looking teacher in
22   this whole school. And I get to sit here just watching
23   you. All of us, we talk about you, well, the guys talk
24   about you. The girls, well, who cares about these girls,
25   they're just —
26   *(Looking at her walk across the room)*
27   Hmmm-mmm-mmm! You are one handsome
28   woman. Where have you been all my life? And this is
29   only September. When it gets colder, you'll be wearing
30   sweaters. Not just pants. And skirts. But sweaters!

1   Tight sweaters. And you'll be up in front of me,
2   walking back and forth, in your sweater, and boots!
3   Oh yeah, I forgot about boots! And what do they
4   call them, those tight black hose things, I love
5   those. I bet you look fantastic in all that stuff. You
6   look good enough today.
7   *(He catches Miss Malton looking at him and he*
8   *quickly starts writing on his notebook.)*
9   Oh please don't ask me again. I won't stare
10   again. I'm doing these figures, I'm paying attention,
11   I'm not thinking about you, no I'm not, no I'm not,
12   just — whew! Saved that time.
13   *(Looking around surreptiously at others in class)*
14   How do these other guys do it? Jim's writing
15   stuff down. He seems to be listening. Alan's looking
16   out the window. Miss Molly Malton could be on his
17   mind. Smart move. Yeah, don't look at her. Stare
18   out the window while you think about taking her
19   home. His eyes just closed. There go his arms.
20   Huh. Yeah, he's holding her all right. Alan, Alan old
21   man, you got the math lady bug too. *(Beat)* Ooohhh,
22   have I got an idea. Why not ask to see Miss Molly
23   after school, here in her classroom, just the two of
24   us. Get a little help with this hypotenuse thing she
25   keeps talking about. Act dumb. *(Beat)* Huh. I wonder
26   if that's a good idea. Dumb may not look very sexy,
27   not to a babe like her. Teacher-type. Hard to
28   remember *(Laughs)* when she looks like that!
29   *(His laugh caught the teacher's attention and his*
30   *cool turns to a stammer.)*
31   Huh? *(Beat)* I'm sorry, I didn't hear you. *(Beat)* I
32   guess I wasn't listening. *(Beat)* No, I wasn't thinking
33   about grammar again, I, I ... I did? I laughed? I, I
34   don't know what I was thinking.
35

Part Four:
Monologs for Guys
(Serious)

We Take Chances

1   *(STUART, 16, alone in a room at a funeral home, comes*
2 *up to his friend Mike, who is lying in a coffin.)*
3   I'm back. They've let me have a few minutes alone
4 with you. Don't worry, I won't try to jump in there with
5 you this time. I, uh, I guess I was more upset than I
6 thought I was, seeing you like this. I'm better today. I
7 don't know if I will stay for the service, hope you don't
8 mind if I don't. *(Beat)* They're kind of busy in this
9 place. I never knew so many people died all the time.
10 There's a funeral going on right now in the church, the
11 chapel, whatever they call it here. Yours is next. After
12 that group clears out.
13   *(Beat)* It's, uh, not as if I have plans for this morning
14 that I can't break. Actually, I was just going to go
15 back home. Hope you don't mind, buddy — I mean, I
16 may come, I just don't know. After yesterday, I'm not
17 sure your parents even want me to come. Scared what
18 I might do next. *(Chuckles.)* Can't blame 'em. I still
19 can't tell you why I tried to get in there with you. Just
20 a reaction, I guess. *(Chuckles again.)* You know us,
21 we've always done everything together, that's what I
22 told Mom. I got quite a look for that one.
23   *(Beat)*
24   I mean, she knew it was true. "We Take Chances."
25 Remember when we came up with that? "W-T-C,
26 Always and Forever." Sounds like a couple of ten-
27 year-olds, doesn't it? I'll never forget it. We were
28 sitting in our tree. That day, we dared each other to
29 climb up higher than we ever had gone before. Past
30 the branch your dad told us never to go above. We got

1 up to this long limb, and sat down, and started to
2 edge out to the end of it. It started to crack, and the
3 next minute, we were in the air, falling on top of it,
4 as it crashed to the ground. It was wonderful! Free-
5 fall! Soaring through the air! I can still feel the air
6 around me. Even with all the other things we've
7 done since. I can still feel that rush.
8   *(Beat)*
9   We were lucky. We were lucky no one was around
10 to see. We would have been grounded forever for
11 that trick.
12   *(Beat)*
13   I'm going to miss you, Mike. I'd be laying out
14 right here beside you if I had been able to go with
15 you. I would have been sliding down that mountain
16 right behind you. W-T-C, Always and Forever.
17   *(Beat)*
18   When I told Mom that I would have gone on the
19 trip with you if I could've afforded it, she started
20 crying. Wouldn't talk to me for a couple hours. When
21 she did, she said, you and I had never been climbing
22 before in our lives. Why would we pick a treacherous
23 climb when we never had even done one? I told her
24 our motto. She wasn't too happy about it, but she
25 understood. Then she said, before you even consider
26 taking another chance like that one, ask yourself if
27 you are at risk. Because if you die, you don't die
28 alone. You take others with you. It's a living hell for
29 anyone you leave behind.
30   *(Beat)*
31   There's something to what she says, Mike. It's
32 rough, really rough, to be here with you, like this.
33   *(Runs out.)*
34
35

Owning Up

1   *(ALLEN, 15, strong and mad, is seated, answering the*
2 *questions of the school principal.)*
3   Hey! How many times do I have to say it, I didn't
4 mean to punch that little guy. He was just, there.
5 *(Beat)* Nah, he hadn't done nothing to me. He was
6 waiting to use the phone, and he would have been
7 better off finding another one. When I hung up, my fist
8 needed to do some travelling, right then, and, well, he
9 was in front of it. If he weren't there, I would've hit the
10 wall instead. *(Beat)* I'm not laughing. Listen, I'm sorry,
11 I told you I was sorry, can't we just leave it at that? It
12 ain't going to happen again.
13   Yeah I was angry! *(Beat)* Yeah, I've been angry
14 before. Yeah, a couple of times. *(Beat)* I don't really see
15 why you care. No one else does. *(Beat)* She does. You're
16 right. My mother cares. But she's the reason that little
17 guy got hit in the first place. *(Beat)* No, I didn't want to
18 hit her — I wish I could have hit him! *(Beat)* No, not the
19 little guy! Him. Him! The big guy. The one I wish I'd
20 never met. Do we really have to go into all this?
21   Okay. Okay! I'll tell you. *(Beat)* I'd been asking my
22 mother all my life to tell me who my father was. She
23 knew, but she wouldn't tell me. Kept saying things like,
24 "When the time is right." Well, lately I'd been asking her
25 again, and finally she says, "I'll come to church with
26 you Sunday. If your father is there, I will introduce
27 you." I couldn't believe it. All this time and my father
28 has been right here beside me all along!? So Sunday
29 came, and we were in church, and I asked her if she
30 had seen him yet. "Hmm-hmmm ... " Man, I didn't

1 hear a word the minister said after that, I was
2 sneaking a look at every man there. When the
3 service was over, mama grabbed my hand and
4 bolted up to the front. One of the elders was stand-
5 ing by the altar, all by himself. She said to him,
6 "Johnny. Johnny, there's someone here I want you
7 to meet. Johnny, this is your son, Allen." I knew
8 this man, I'd seen him in church every Sunday. He
9 sits with his wife. And his children, three of them,
10 but none of them were around. There was no one
11 there but us. "Don't you go trying to pin him on me,
12 Ella girl. You get that right out of your mind!" That's
13 all he said. And he walked off.
14   Mama called him later and asked him to take a
15 blood test to prove I was not his child. She finally
16 got him to say yes. I went to the clinic the next day.
17 He sent his blood over. The results were due back
18 today. I called home, and got the news. That little
19 guy was just standing there, waiting to use the
20 phone after me. Not a match! That's what they
21 said, not a match.
22   I look a lot like this Johnny. He pulled a fast one
23 on me again. Like I said, he sent his blood over to
24 the lab. Didn't have it taken there. No, because
25 then things wouldn't have worked out the way he
26 planned. He's a big honcho. Got his own business.
27 Family. He doesn't need me. He doesn't want me.
28 *(Takes a fist and plows it into his other hand.)* It makes
29 me so mad.
30
31
32
33
34
35

No More Basketball

1   (MARCUS, 16, in a wheelchair, rolls out quickly and
2   comes to a sudden stop. Lowers head, fighting back both
3   tears and anger. It is a long time before he can compose
4   himself to speak. He speaks to a girlfriend who has been
5   waiting for him in an outpatient clinic.)
6   Don't touch me. Don't touch me! Don't go. Don't
7   go. (A long beat) They said ... they said, no more. No
8   more basketball. Not ever. They said the, the uh, the
9   bullet went through something in my spine which can
10 never grow back together. Some kind of nerve thing.
11 It's almost cut through, but not all the way. Don't
12 touch me! They put me down for therapy, here at the
13 hospital, every day but Sunday. They said I might be
14 able to walk, but it would always be slow. Real slow. I
15 could kill Harry! If I had a gun this minute, I, I ... he'd
16 better not put his face anywhere I can see it. I told him
17 we shouldn't go there! But Harry had to go ... "That's
18 where the action is, man!" (Beat) Don't look at me like
19 that. It was Harry's idea! (Beat) Yeah, I knew there'd
20 been fights there. I, I ... you know, you figure you're
21 not involved, the bullet's not aimed at you, so you'll be
22 okay.
23   (He shifts in the chair.)
24   It hurts. They said it was going to hurt. They can
25 give me some painkillers, but they said I should try to
26 get used to it instead because it isn't ever going to go
27 away. They said it's going to hurt every time I take a
28 step. And even when I don't, I'll feel it. They said it
29 would hurt real bad if I moved around a lot, like if I
30 played ball.

1   *(Raises his arm deliberately.)*
2   They said I was lucky! Lucky that I got out alive.
3   Lucky that I could move my arms. If I were so
4   almighty lucky, I never would have taken that bullet!
5   *(Slams his fist.)* I might as well be dead!
6   *(At that point again where anger easily turns into self-*
7   *pity and tears; has to catch himself to keep from crying.)*
8   Basketball's the only thing I ever wanted to do.
9   There's never been anything else — it's always been
10   making it with the ball. Going to college on the ball.
11   Making the majors. Making the money. Doing what
12   I want to do.
13   *(Beat)*
14   I didn't really want to go to that club. It wasn't
15   my idea. I just went along. And look where it got
16   me. I haven't ever been in a hospital before. All
17   those years playing ball, nothing's ever happened to
18   me that I had to come someplace like this.
19   *(Beat)*
20   One of the doctors said something — the other
21   one said I shouldn't count on it. Anyway, this one
22   doctor said he had treated a guy who had broken his
23   neck diving, and there was no chance he would ever
24   walk again. And that guy would come to therapy like
25   he was in training or something — do ten times as
26   much as they told him to do. He kept at it every day
27   until they had to pick him up off the floor. The doc
28   said he's okay now — running, swimming, doing all
29   that stuff again. They said he'd never make it, but
30   he did. That's what I'm gonna do. That's what I
31   gotta do.
32   *(Starts rolling away.)*
33   Wanna see where I'll be?
34
35

Mom's Getting Married Again

1   (*JACKSON, 14, in the middle of talking to his best friend*)
2   He's crazy, I tell you. Last night you know what he
3 fixed us for supper? These huge slabs of beef, with a
4 side of spaghetti? He called it something else, it was
5 all dripping with cream and butter and cheese and
6 eggs even! All this stuff they tell you not to eat. Well I
7 ate it. I hated to insult the guy, and well, I have to
8 admit it tasted good, but like I said to Mom after
9 dinner, "What's he trying to do? Kill us with choles-
10 terol?" And she laughed! I don't know. She seems to
11 be in love with him or something ... I don't really know
12 what it is, but I do know that I'm not about to live with
13 that guy.
14   And there's Carol. I mean, you think she wants to
15 live with Mom and me? She doesn't even talk to me.
16 Never has. Just passes in the hall like she doesn't
17 even see me. I told Mom, what do I need with another
18 sister? I mean, isn't one enough? You know what she
19 said? She said, "Cindy's practically grown. In the new
20 house, we might not even have a room for her, not if
21 she gets that job in Dallas." What? Is this what Mom's
22 going to do to me as soon as I get a little job some-
23 where? Throw me out? All right all right, don't tell me,
24 Cindy's twenty-two, in college, never comes back home
25 much anyway, but still, don't you think ... well, never
26 mind, that's not the most important thing here.
27   I tell you Mom's going a bit nutso with this getting
28 married again and I gotta do something before it gets
29 way out of hand. So let me try this idea out on you,
30 huh? I mean, let me tell you what I plan to tell Mom

1 tonight. I need to practice it, so I'll get it right.
2 Okay? Thanks. Okay, here goes. I mean, you know
3 I'm gonna talk to you now as if you were Mom.
4 Right. Just assume she, you, we are sitting at the
5 table, we've had dinner, and you're in a good mood,
6 I mean I won't say any of this unless she's in a good
7 mood. Maybe I'll clear the table, yeah, that's a good
8 idea. Okay, so I've cleared the table, and I sit back
9 down and I say ...
10   "Mom. I've been thinking about you getting mar-
11 ried to Bill, and I've been trying to imagine what it
12 will be like here at home. Please ... " *(Aside)* I know
13 she will interrupt me there, so I'll hold up my hand,
14 like this and say — "Please, just let me tell you
15 what I've been thinking. Okay? Well, we're not going
16 to have a lot of meals like this, just the two of us.
17 In fact, our whole life is going to be turned upside
18 down with all these other people in the house all the
19 time, and, you know, it's going to be hard on them,
20 too. I mean, Carol's not used to having another kid
21 around either. So, I have this idea. Please, let me
22 get it all out." *(Aside)* She'll be like that, wanting to
23 tell me how it's going to be all right before I even get
24 a chance to tell her the idea. "So, my idea is this.
25 After the wedding, why don't you and me stay right
26 here, and Carol and her Dad can stay in his house,
27 and every so often he can come over here for awhile,
28 or you can go over and stay with him. I mean I'd be
29 all right by myself for a day or two. Maybe even a
30 week! And I'm sure Carol would be too. And then
31 we can all go on just like we have been, and no one
32 would have to be upset. And the two of you can be
33 together whenever you want. Separate houses. I'd
34 like that. Wouldn't you?"
35

The Visit

1   *(TODD, 16, has just walked into the visiting room of a*
2 *prison, to see his father. He watches a door anxiously and*
3 *fingers a small camera. A man comes in, TODD waves,*
4 *then watches as the man comes close. Speaks as if talking*
5 *to his father, who would sit opposite him, with a screen*
6 *dividing them.)*
7   **I'm Todd. I thought maybe you wouldn't recognize**
8 **me.** *(Beat)* **Yeah. Big. That's what Mom says.** *(Beat,*
9 *listening to Dad's question)* **She's okay.** *(Nervous laugh)*
10 **She said you wouldn't ask about her.** *(Beat, listening)*
11 **Sure, yeah, I'll tell her you did.** *(Beat)* **Why'd I come?**
12 **Well, I — oh that's why you asked about her? You**
13 **thought something was wrong? And I had to come to**
14 **tell you? No, no, she's fine. Everyone's just fine. Well,**
15 **that is, everyone I know, maybe not everyone you**
16 **know.** *(Beat)* **Or knew.** *(Beat, listening)* **Not that I know**
17 **of. I haven't heard of anyone dying, that I knew. So,**
18 **how've you been? Do they treat you all right in here?**
19 *(Beat, listens, nervous laugh.)* **Well, yeah, a jail's a jail,**
20 **I guess.** *(Beat)* **How long have you been in here?** *(Beat)*
21 **Really ... Gee.**
22   *(Beat, listens.)*
23   **No, I didn't know what, I mean, where — no one**
24 **would tell me where you were for the longest time. I'd**
25 **always get some answer like, "Oh, he's a long way**
26 **away, we couldn't possibly go there today." That was**
27 **Grandma's usual line. Mom's was, "Don't ask me that**
28 **again, Todd. I don't want to have to hit you."** *(Beat, listens.)*
29 **No, not in a long while. I'm too big for her to hit now.**
30 **And, I guess I stopped asking. You get pretty busy**

1   with school and camp and karate and all that stuff.
2   I got a job, after school, and I can work there full-
3   time this summer if I want it. I had to fill out an
4   application, and they asked for the name and
5   addresses of you and mom, and this time, when I
6   asked her, she gave me an envelope with this
7   address on it, from some letter you had sent her.
8   The postmark was ... ten years ago. I was sure you
9   wouldn't be here, but she said she would have
10 heard if you weren't.
11   *(Beat, listens.)*
12   I, I just came to visit. Do you mind? *(Beat)* I really
13 didn't have anything I had to tell you, I just, I just
14 ... I don't think I have seen you since ... I think I was
15 five. There was this day the school secretary came
16 to class, Miss Michael's class, so that was kinder-
17 garten. The secretary took me to the office, and you
18 were there, with the principal, and you told me
19 "good-bye," and that I wouldn't see you "for a while,"
20 and that I'd "be the man of the family," and "to be
21 nice to Mom." You left, and Miss Michael was right
22 outside the door and she took me back to class. I
23 held that picture in my mind, of you, standing in
24 front of me there, in that office, for as long as I
25 could. It's the only picture I had of you, the one in
26 my mind, there aren't any in the house. And when
27 I was filling out the job application, I realized I
28 couldn't see you anymore. The picture in my mind
29 was gone. It wasn't just fuzzy or dim, you were gone!
30 So I got to thinking, I'd like to see you. I needed a
31 picture of you again. And, I don't know, I guess I
32 thought you might like to see me. I mean, I'm not
33 five anymore. *(Beat, listens.)* Oh, no, no trouble.
34 Yeah, sure, that's fine. Be seeing you, too. *(Watches*
35 *Dad leave. Puts camera away.)*

No Other Place to Go

1   *(DARREN, 16, talking to his parents, who have just*
2 *demanded that he tell them where he's been going after school)*
3   It's not what you think. I mean I don't really know
4 what you think, but nothing so bad that you should
5 ground me. I've been meaning to tell you, but ... I've
6 got a job. That's all it is, a job. There's nothing the
7 matter with it, I'm over at the _____ *(insert name of*
8 *local grocery store.),* stocking shelves. They've got me
9 back in the dairy, so you probably wouldn't see me if
10 you came in. I go right from school and then I come
11 home for supper. *(Beat)* I didn't think you'd miss me. I
12 mean, you're not home, and I am sixteen — *(Beat, Mom*
13 *interrupts.)* When have you called? I, I didn't think you'd
14 have anything to worry about. I'm sorry I didn't tell you.
15   *(Beat, Dad has a question.)*
16   I guess it is my first job, yeah ... I didn't really think
17 about it that way, I just started working one day, and
18 after three hours, it didn't seem like a big deal. Pretty
19 ordinary stuff. Pretty ordinary place. It's not as if I had-
20 n't been to a grocery before. *(Beat, question)*
21   Minimum wage. Not a lot. *(Beat)* Well, I've been ...
22 I've — *(Beat)* No, nothing's gone to the bank. *(Beat)* No,
23 there's nothing I really needed to buy. *(Beat)* I'm not
24 saving it for anything. *(Beat)* I am not buying drugs!
25   *(Very long beat, didn't want to tell them this)*
26   I've been giving it away. It's just fifteen dollars a
27 day, it's not very much, but I've got a friend that
28 needs it, and that's why I'm working. *(Beat)* She's per-
29 fectly well — *(Beat)* I didn't get anyone pregnant!
30   *(Very long beat)*

1   I've been giving it to Darlene. Darlene from
2   church. I know you don't like her, but — *(Beat)*
3   Yeah, that's right. She had the kid, last summer,
4   but did you know her parents threw her out? Well,
5   they did. So she was living with the baby's dad, he's
6   got this trailer, and she was trying to still come to
7   school. I ran into her in the hall. She had her arm
8   in a sling, and had dropped some stuff, so I was
9   helping her pick it up, and she started crying. She
10   said to me, "Darren, I really need a Coke." We used
11   to go for Cokes all the time, in between Sunday
12   school and church. Anyway, it was the end of the
13   day, and so we went across the street for a Coke.
14   She finally told me why she was crying. He had
15   broken her arm. Just the day before. She didn't
16   want to live with him, but she didn't have anywhere
17   else to go. No one else would take care of the baby
18   while she was in school. And now she hated to leave
19   him alone with the baby — after what he did to her.
20   Said she was going to have to quit school, and she
21   was scared about spending more time cooped up
22   with him in the trailer. She didn't have any other
23   place to go. I felt real bad for her. I'd been thinking
24   about doing something after school anyway, so I
25   asked her if she could find a place for a couple hun-
26   dred dollars a month. I could give her that ... if I
27   could earn it. I'll never forget that moment for as
28   long as I live. She had a look on her face that I will
29   always see whenever I need to feel good. *(Beat)* Dar-
30   lene found a bedroom for her and the baby. It's in a
31   house, with a woman who takes care of other kids
32   during the day. Right there, in her house. So the
33   baby's okay too. And Darlene's finishing school. It's
34   kinda our little secret. Do you mind?
35

The Boss's Son

1   (GIL, 16, just finishing his bag lunch, and can of soda.
2   Talking to himself, still embarrassed about what happened
3   at work)
4   The question is, do I have the nerve to go back to
5   the warehouse? (Sigh, beat) Or, then there's the other
6   question, do I really have a choice? (Sigh) If I don't go
7   back to work, I might as well leave home. Don't exactly
8   want to leave home. Can't afford to leave home. I like
9   home. I should've found another job. This was just so
10   easy — didn't have to put on a shirt and tie for an
11   interview, didn't have to go to some strange place,
12   didn't have to impress somebody I didn't know. When
13   Mom said working for family has its own problems, I
14   thought maybe she meant I wouldn't get paid on time,
15   or maybe Dad would be watching me every minute. I
16   wasn't expecting to be embarrassed like this.
17   I can't believe I left the tap running last night. I
18   can't believe that much glue can drip out just
19   overnight. That spill is going to take weeks to clean
20   up. Dad may have to pay overtime so we can get it up
21   before it cures into a permanently immovable mass.
22   The accident with the forklift was bad enough — I
23   can't believe I didn't hear the arms dragging against
24   the side of the building — that motor is louder than I
25   thought. At least I didn't cut through the warehouse
26   wall. But still, somebody will have to paint that gash,
27   otherwise it will rust. But we're spending all our spare
28   time cleaning up my glue spill instead. It will be weeks
29   before someone can fix the wall.
30   Why do I do these things? And it's been like this

1 from the very start. That first week — filled the
2 drums with glue, sealed them off, moved them to
3 the bay for pick up, and then forgot to bill the
4 customer. Gave somebody five drums of free glue!
5 Can't remember whose order it was. Can't find the
6 invoice. Probably threw it away. Why? Why do I do
7 these things?
8   Dad's right. My mind is elsewhere. I do live for
9 the breaks. Gotta make my calls, get my evening
10 together, reach out to the world! Any excuse not to
11 work. And here I am talking to myself, putting off
12 going back. *(Looks at watch.)* Late! Again! I shouldn't
13 leave for lunch, but it feels so good to get out. Every
14 time I turn around I do something else wrong! Am I
15 dumb or something? How does Dad do it? How does
16 he keep his mind on the job? Well, for one thing, he
17 doesn't do what I've been doing. He isn't filling the
18 drums anymore. He isn't cleaning the walls. He isn't
19 running the forklift. He's in the air-conditioned office
20 instead of the warehouse. He gets out. Sees
21 customers. Eats lunch with friends. I wonder what
22 he really thinks of me ... *(Beat)* That was kinda
23 sweet what Joe said. That I'm no different from any
24 other summer hire — other kids made the same
25 mistakes I have. Everyone he's seen. I don't
26 remember ever hearing about glue hardening all
27 over the warehouse floor, but maybe it happened.
28 Maybe Joe's already said that to Dad. Maybe he
29 isn't mad at me. Maybe, maybe. Maybe I should go
30 back and face the music. I can always promise him
31 I'll try real hard to do better. Again.
32
33
34
35

He's No Friend of Mine

1   (HOWARD, 16, at home with a friend, and currently on
2 phone)
3   He did? He did? Oh he did … Well let me tell you
4 something and you hear it straight, because this is
5 Howard Kerster talking to you, and not his "good
6 friend" Jim Peters telling you what he wants you to
7 think I said. I've never given anyone permission to
8 sign my name. No, I don't want to speak to him. I
9 don't care what he says, I don't care what you do with
10 him, but let me tell you, he's no friend of mine.
11   (Hangs up, turns to friend in room with him.)
12   Unbelievable! Peters is down at the club, trying to
13 get lunch on my parents' card. Trying to sign my name!
14 Telling the waiter that I was supposed to meet him
15 there, and he didn't know what could have happened
16 to me, but he's hungry and wants to go ahead and
17 order. The nerve of the guy! He just signed my name!
18 Nobody recognized him, and that's why they called. I
19 mean he might have got away with it … Eating there!
20 Without any of us! On our card! (Beat) I think he went
21 with us once. He was, uh, over here at the house,
22 somebody else was here too, was it you? (Beat) Maybe
23 Allen. I don't remember, but it was time for dinner, so
24 my folks took us to the club to eat. It was Allen,
25 because Peters came over to the house with him, and
26 I was kinda mad at Allen for bringing somebody along.
27 We were supposed to be doing this history project
28 together, so Peters was in the way. Allen told me later
29 he tried to get rid of him, told him we had to work and
30 all and that he'd be bored just sitting around watching

1 us, but he tagged along anyway.
2   I don't think he has any friends, I mean real
3 friends. Allen didn't want him. I guess we felt kinda
4 sorry for the guy, he was just there, you know what
5 I mean? And you know, now I remember, at dinner
6 he kept saying all this stupid stuff to my parents.
7 You know, like, uh, "This is the best steak, I've ever
8 had, Mrs. Kerster," or asking how long they'd been
9 members, or whether they ate at the club every
10 week, just all sorts of stuff that had nothing to do
11 with what we were talking about.
12   He was kinda funny like that when I met him. He
13 came up behind me one day in the hall, I was at the
14 water fountain, and he said, "Aren't you Howard
15 Kerster?" and he told me he was a friend of Allen's,
16 and that Allen had told him all sorts of stuff about
17 me, and then he started asking me all these
18 questions like where I lived, and had I lived here all
19 my life, and did I know so and so, I can't even
20 remember all the people he asked if I knew. Oh, but
21 I remember one. Molly Elmore. She came up to me
22 in church, mad as a hornet. *(Like Molly)* "Your friend
23 Jim Peters said you told him to ask me out. Next
24 time, why don't you take the trouble to introduce
25 me first!" *(Beat)* Yeah, I'd been wanting to go out
26 with her myself, but uh, she's still cooling down
27 from that. *(Beat)* Peters used me, you know? With
28 Molly. And at the club. You think he wants you as a
29 friend, you even feel a little sorry for him 'cause he
30 doesn't seem to have any, but then he goes and
31 plays you cheap. Uses your name. Lies! Nope, he's
32 nooo friend of mine. *(Picks up phone.)* I'm going to
33 call them back. I want to be sure they threw him out.
34
35

School's a Breeze Compared to This

1   *(NICK, 17, in bed at night. His Dad's in the bed next to*
2 *his. NICK's body aches so much, he can't sleep.)*
3   *(Tries one position.)* **Ow!** *(Then another)* **Ooowwww!**
4 **Dad? Dad? You awake? Dead to the world. Where I**
5 **should be. Sixteen-hour days. Six sixteen-hour days in**
6 **a row. Unbelievable. My neck is killing me!** *(Shifts.)* **My**
7 **back is one big blister. There's no more aspirin in the**
8 **house and every muscle in my body is hollering for**
9 **pain killers.** *(Looking over at Dad)* **He must be used to**
10 **it. He's not even moving. Maybe that's the trick.** *(Tries*
11 *position like a corpse laid out.)* **AAAggghhh!** *(Sits up.)*
12 **'Course he doesn't have a sunburn either.**
13   **It's your own fault, stupid. Up on a roof, in the sun,**
14 **from six in the morning. Oh yeah, take your shirt off,**
15 **Instant tan! I should have put the sunscreen on.** *(Beat)*
16 **I would have sweated it off in a minute. Would have**
17 **had to keep putting more cream on all afternoon. The**
18 **whole crew would have laughed their heads off every**
19 **time I pulled out the tube. I'm the butt of their jokes**
20 **enough, having to learn everything from the bottom**
21 **up. Those guys are brutal. Sure would hate to have a**
22 **job like this without Dad around.** *(Leg cramps up.)*
23 **Damn!** *(Rubs it.)* **Work is brutal.**
24   **One day a week to recover. I'll sleep all day. If I**
25 **ever get to sleep. I'm never going to see any of my**
26 **friends. Great. I move here so I can see my friends,**
27 **and I haven't talked to anyone all week. No one but**
28 **Dad. And the crew. They're not worth much. Next**
29 **week will be more of the same. I should have asked**
30 **Dad what the hours were going to be. I might have**

1   stayed with Mom. And graduated.

2   Just one more semester. Four months. Four
3   months of this, and I'll be dead. I'll have calluses on
4   my fingers. And skin cancer. And I won't have seen
5   my friends because they have to do homework on
6   Sunday night. The only night I have off.

7   *(Beat, bolts upright.)*

8   I've only missed five days! Five days. You get
9   that many sick days. I could go back to Mom's
10   tomorrow, and be in school on Monday morning. If
11   Dad could drive me. Dad? Dad? *(Beat)* He's not
12   going to want to hit the road tomorrow. Eight hours
13   to Mom's? Even worse. Sixteen for him. He's got to
14   be back to start the other crew on a roof Monday
15   morning. He's not going to want to do it.

16   *(Beat)*

17   I could fly! I got the money he owes me for working
18   this week, I could pay for it myself! He'd like that.
19   It wouldn't cost him anything extra. *(Beat)* School. I
20   can't believe it sounds so easy. Only seven hours a
21   day. Mostly sitting. Half the afternoon off. Saturdays
22   and Sundays free. *(Beat, looks over at Dad.)* He'll be
23   mad. "Just like everything else you do," that's what
24   he'll say. "You start something, but you don't finish."
25   *(Beat)* This is hard work, Dad, this job of yours.
26   Now that I think about it, I'd really rather finish
27   school. If I put it like that, he might not get so mad.
28   *(Lies back down to sleep.)*
29
30
31
32
33
34
35

What a Babe!

1   (ARNOLD, 16, seated beside his friend Little-T at a table
2 in a restaurant. Little-T's mother just got up from the table
3 and left for the ladies room. ARNOLD's eyes follow her until
4 she is out of sight.)
5   Hmmm-Hmmm. Hmmm-mmm-mmm. Hmmm!
6 (Turns to Little-T.) **My dad has a word for that. Hot.** (Like
7 his dad) **"So hot you don't care if you get burned, you
8 just want to get as close as you can." You see it? She
9 makes you want to follow her wherever she is going,
10 right into the ladies room, in front of a car, off a cliff.
11 Now that's a dangerous woman, don't you think? I tell
12 you she is as hot as they come, man, Wow! I mean,
13 great legs, cute little figure on her, lots of girls you
14 and I both know, buddy, would kill for a body put
15 together like that one, but it's all those smiles and
16 looks that say "Come on, Arnold, come on, I want to
17 play!" Girls at school, they haven't learned half the
18 stuff she does just naturally! You know me, I've
19 always liked the girls a couple grades up, right? Hey,
20 I don't need to tell you, but you know, now that I see
21 this one, maybe I need to move on to older women. I
22 mean, she's like nobody's mother I've ever met. You're
23 one sly fellow, Little-T, keeping her all to yourself. Not
24 one word have I ever heard about that little mother of
25 yours, not one word from anybody!**
26   (Just a breath of a beat, this is an almost non-stop
27 monolog and you can imagine Little-T is astonished at first
28 and then builds a slow-burn.)
29   **You know, I get the idea maybe you can't see her
30 proper, being as she's your mother and all. I'm no**

1 expert about mothers — mine was never around,
2 but dames I know. My dad taught me everything
3 there is to know. And my mother, she taught me
4 too, in her way.
5 *(Breath of a beat)*
6 Never knew her, never laid eyes on her, never
7 saw even so much as a tiny little black and white
8 picture of her. She walked out on us, taking every-
9 thing she owned, every letter, every photograph,
10 everything that even had a trace of her. She left Dad
11 holding me and the diaper bag. That's how he tells it.
12 And I never heard any different, not from anybody.
13 We never moved. If she ever wanted to find me, I
14 was right where she left me. But she's never come
15 around. Not that Dad's been hurting.
16 *(Beat)*
17 He's had lots of women, I mean blondes, red-
18 heads, blue-eyes, those big brown doe-eyes, those
19 were my favorites, but every one of them a good-
20 looker. And always one woman at a time. That I
21 knew of anyway. Of course, a kid doesn't catch on
22 to everything, even I know that. I asked Dad once
23 why didn't any of these women want to stay with
24 us, and he said they didn't need us, that they all
25 had places of their own to go home to. He said it was
26 just him and me, and was there anything I was
27 missing? "Dames you only need for one thing" — he
28 says that a lot. 'Course I never knew what he meant
29 for a long time. He wasn't about to tell me either —
30 "You'll know what it is when you need it." Hmmm,
31 hmmm. She oughta be on her way back pretty soon.
32 So tell me Little-T, what's your mom's name again?
33
34
35

Don't Ever Look at Her Again!

1   *(LITTLE-T, 16, at restaurant table, turns to his best friend*
2 *Arnold, sitting beside him, who has just been ogling LITTLE-*
3 *T's mother. This monolog could follow "What a Babe!")*
4   I don't believe what I just heard! What do you
5 think we're talking about here? My mother is Mrs.
6 Roberts to you. Now. And forever! You're leaving, man
7 — we don't want your face anymore for dinner. You're
8 getting out of here before Mom comes back from the
9 ladies room.
10   *(Beat)*
11   No, wait a minute! Arnold. Let me be sure we're
12 clear on this. Don't you ever look at her like that
13 again! You hear me? Don't you ever, ever, let me catch
14 you looking at, or talking about, my mother like she
15 was some piece of meat! Am I getting through? Am I
16 getting into that brain-damaged skull of yours?
17   *(All he can do not to hit Arnold)*
18   No matter what she looks like to you, she's no
19 chick. No little girlie. Not some spread in Playboy, not
20 a babe, not a dame. She's my mother! She's real!
21 She's married! And you've met my Dad, remember
22 him?
23   *(Beat)*
24   Arnold, it's like I don't know you tonight. I've never
25 seen you like this. I mean, I've been around you with
26 girls at school and all, but ... Believe me, if I knew you
27 were going to come on to my mother, I wouldn't have
28 asked you to come with us tonight. You understand?
29 Whatever you've been thinking about my mother,
30 Arnold, if you can't get it out of your mind this

1 instant, you can find yourself some other friend. You
2 think she asked me to invite you, you in particular,
3 to come with us? She doesn't know you from Adam.
4 She told me I could bring someone along if I wanted.
5 Any one of my friends would have been just fine
6 with her.
7   *(Beat)*
8   I like my mom. I like her a lot. When I was a kid,
9 I used to think I had the best mother in the world. I
10 used to run all the way home from school because
11 I could hardly wait to tell her what had happened
12 that day. She was just the same then as she is
13 today. She'd see me, and she'd be all smiles. She'd
14 be just like she's been with you here tonight. And
15 believe me, those aren't come-on-I-want-to-play
16 smiles you're getting from her. She's listening to
17 you. She's interested in what you're doing. That's
18 just the way she is. She's like that with my dad.
19 She's like that with my sister. She's just treating
20 you like she treats everyone else. Believe me, she
21 doesn't want to hop into bed with you.
22   *(Beat, looks and sees his mother.)*
23   She's coming back. Get out of here. I'll tell her
24 something, Don't worry, she'll be sympathetic.
25   *(Arnold on way out)*
26   And, Arnold? Don't even think about asking
27 Mary out. My sister's not a babe either.
28   *(Beat)*
29   Oh, hi Mom.
30   *(Beat)*
31   He got a call. Had to leave. Don't worry, I'll eat
32 his shrimp.
33
34
35

The Choice

1 *(SAM, 14, filling out a form)*
2 So. Next year I can go to Central High in town, or
3 I can go out here to Pine Grove. This is cool. Why didn't
4 they give me a choice for seventh grade? I never would
5 have failed algebra if I could have gotten away from
6 Mister Hammer. He was one mean teacher. Yeah, I
7 would have changed schools as soon as I saw his face.
8 *(Writing on form)* "Sam Jamison, 1914 South 80th
9 Street. Age, 14." *(Reading)* "Enter the name of the
10 high school you wish to attend." *(Pen still in hand, but
11 he doesn't write this in.)* Pine Grove Senior High.
12 Why wouldn't I go to Pine Grove? I'll know everyone
13 there. They all live around here. Jason and Carl and
14 Van, they've already signed up. They wrote down Pine
15 Grove. The kids at church all go to Pine Grove. Why
16 wouldn't I go to Pine Grove? Just because I have a
17 choice I wouldn't go where all my friends were? What
18 am I, crazy? Central's an hour away. An hour on a
19 bus. I'd have to get out of the house by six fifteen just
20 to get on the bus. Of course, I might get a car. Not
21 the first year, no, but even if I did, it still takes time
22 to drive. I like to sleep. Sam, you like to sleep as late
23 as you can. *(Pen in hand again)* Pine Grove Senior High.
24 *(But he can't bring himself to write it in.)*
25 Why'd they have to give us a choice? Matt's dad
26 sure made it easy for him. Pine Grove, no choice about
27 it, but that's because his dad didn't want him mixing
28 with the kids up at Central. Okay, so the kids at
29 Central aren't exactly like the kids out here. I mean,
30 they come from pretty near downtown. But, let me tell

115

1 you, I went to one of Central's shows last year, and
2 it was way better than anything Pine Grove ever put
3 on. I mean, well, okay, I like to act. I like to sing.
4 I've been in the summer musicals at the park ever
5 since I was eight. But still, at Central, last year,
6 they did A Chorus Line, and I tell you, they knocked
7 us flat in our chairs. The sound that came out off
8 that stage was ... well, you just wouldn't have
9 believed what those kids did! *(Hums and dances a*
10 *few bars of "One Singular Sensation.")* They say the
11 drama teacher there worked in New York. Was
12 in shows and everything. Back-stage, on-stage,
13 directing, you name it. He goes back in the
14 summer, and learns all the latest tricks. I've been
15 to New York once. When I was ten. I'd go back in a
16 minute, too. *(Picks up pen.)* Central High School.
17 *(Still doesn't actually write it.)*
18   Matt might not ever talk to me again if I put
19 down Central. Carl? I don't know. Van, Van might
20 not mind so much, but Jason, it won't be pretty
21 with Jason. He'll never stop talking about it, all
22 summer long. Of course, what I could do is not tell
23 them anything until right before school starts. They
24 might not even ask ... Yeah, right! It will definitely
25 come up. So. Is it worth it? A summer, a whole
26 summer, without any friends. Well, next summer
27 the drama club at Central might go to New York.
28 They've done that before, too. Pine Grove never
29 goes anywhere. I don't care, *(Writes)* Central ... High
30 ... School. I just got to do it. If they're really my
31 friends, they'll understand.
32
33
34
35

About the Author

Diana Howie has written eight full-length plays in the past ten years, and has seen seven of them produced. Like these monologs, three of her plays, *The Brightest Light, Susanna of Stratford,* and *Judy's Friend,* use real people (Alexander Hamilton, Susanna Shakespeare and Judy Garland) as characters. Characters in her other plays are inspired by people she has known, but are essentially fictional creations. "I'm usually not even thinking of writing a play," she says. "Something a person does catches my interest, and pretty soon I am trying to imagine why they did that, and the story evolves."

Before taking up writing full-time, Ms. Howie was a reference librarian in New Jersey libraries. Since moving to Texas, she has completed undergraduate and graduate studies in theatre, and was fortunate to have studied in Houston with Jose Quintero, a legendary director of new work for the stage. Ms. Howie has been Playwright in Residence of the Country Playhouse since 1997, and is a teaching artist in elementary schools, introducing theatre to about 500 students each school year. She is a member of The Dramatists Guild.

Order Form

Meriwether Publishing Ltd.
P.O. Box 7710
Colorado Springs, CO 80933
Telephone: (719) 594-4422
Website: www.meriwetherpublishing.com

Please send me the following books:

_____ **Tight Spots #BK-B233** $14.95
by Diana Howie
True-to-life monolog characterizations for student actors

_____ **The Flip Side #BK-B221** $14.95
by Heather H. Henderson
64 point-of-view monologs for teens

_____ **Winning Monologs for Young Actors** $14.95
#BK-B127
by Peg Kehret
Honest-to-life monologs for young actors

_____ **Encore! More Winning Monologs for** $14.95
Young Actors #BK-B144
by Peg Kehret
More honest-to-life monologs for young actors

_____ **Acting Natural #BK-B133** $14.95
by Peg Kehret
Honest-to-life monologs, dialogs and playlets for teens

_____ **Get in the Act! #BK-B104** $14.95
by Shirley Ullom
Monologs, dialogs and skits for teens

_____ **Theatre Games for Young Performers #BK-B188** $16.95
by Maria C. Novelly
Improvisations and exercises for developing acting skills

These and other fine Meriwether Publishing books are available at
your local bookstore or direct from the publisher. Use the handy
order form on this page.

Name: _____

Organization name: _____

Address: _____

City: _____ State: _____

Zip: _____ Phone: _____

❑ **Check Enclosed**
❑ **Visa or MasterCard #** _____
                                            Expiration
Signature: _____ *date:* _____
          (required for Visa/MasterCard orders)

COLORADO RESIDENTS: Please add 3% sales tax.
SHIPPING: Include $2.75 for the first book and 50¢ for each additional book ordered.

❑ *Please send me a copy of your complete catalog of books and plays.*

Order Form

Meriwether Publishing Ltd.
P.O. Box 7710
Colorado Springs, CO 80933
Telephone: (719) 594-4422
Website: www.meriwetherpublishing.com

Please send me the following books:

_____ **Tight Spots   #BK-B233** $14.95
by Diana Howie
True-to-life monolog characterizations for student actors

_____ **The Flip Side   #BK-B221** $14.95
by Heather H. Henderson
64 point-of-view monologs for teens

_____ **Winning Monologs for Young Actors** $14.95
#BK-B127
by Peg Kehret
Honest-to-life monologs for young actors

_____ **Encore! More Winning Monologs for** $14.95
Young Actors   #BK-B144
by Peg Kehret
More honest-to-life monologs for young actors

_____ **Acting Natural   #BK-B133** $14.95
by Peg Kehret
Honest-to-life monologs, dialogs and playlets for teens

_____ **Get in the Act!   #BK-B104** $14.95
by Shirley Ullom
Monologs, dialogs and skits for teens

_____ **Theatre Games for Young Performers   #BK-B188** $16.95
by Maria C. Novelly
Improvisations and exercises for developing acting skills

These and other fine Meriwether Publishing books are available at
your local bookstore or direct from the publisher. Use the handy
order form on this page.

Name: _____

Organization name: _____

Address: _____

City: _____ State: _____

Zip: _____ Phone: _____

❑ Check Enclosed
❑ Visa or MasterCard # _____
                                          Expiration
Signature: _____ *date:* _____
        (required for Visa/MasterCard orders)

COLORADO RESIDENTS: Please add 3% sales tax.
SHIPPING: Include $2.75 for the first book and 50¢ for each additional book ordered.

❑ *Please send me a copy of your complete catalog of books and plays.*